WRITE
SOURCE

Daily Language
Workouts

Grade 10

Daily MUG Shot Sentences
Weekly MUG Shot Paragraphs
Sentence Combining
Daily Writing Practice
Journals and Learning Logs

a daily language and
writing program

for **Level 10**

WRITE SOURCE.®

GREAT SOURCE EDUCATION GROUP
a Houghton Mifflin Company
Wilmington, Massachusetts
www.greatsource.com

A Few Words About
Daily Language Workouts 10

Before you begin . . .

The activities in this book will help your students build basic writing, editing, and proofreading skills. You'll find three types of exercises on the following pages.

MUG Shot Sentences, Paragraphs, and Sentence Combining There are 150 sentences and 30 paragraphs highlighting **m**echanics, **u**sage, and **g**rammar errors for students to correct. The MUG Shot sentences can be used daily; the paragraphs should be used once a week. The sentence combining activities that follow each paragraph provide students with additional writing practice.

Daily Writing Practice This section contains **writing prompts** that you can photocopy or make into a transparency. The **Show-Me sentences** provide starting points for paragraphs, essays, and a wide variety of other forms. They also provide opportunities for students to *show* rather than *tell*. The **sentence modeling** section helps students improve their writing style.

Journals and Learning Logs The journals and learning logs section contains guidelines and starting points for journal writing. Students will also find guidelines for learning logs and note taking.

Authors: Pat Sebranek and Dave Kemper

Printed in the United States of America

International Standard Book Number: 978-0-669-53163-3
International Standard Book Number: 0-669-53163-4

1 2 3 4 5 6 7 8 9 10 -POO- 10 09 08 07 06

CONTENTS

Editing and Proofreading Marks

Use the following symbols to correct each MUG Shot sentence and paragraph.

Insert here.	∧	*them* take ∧ home
Insert a comma, semicolon, or colon.	∧, ∧; ∧:	Troy ∧, Michigan
Insert a period.	⊙	Mrs ⊙
Insert a hyphen or a dash.	-∧ ‾∧	one ∧- third cup
Insert a question mark or an exclamation point.	?∧ !∧	How about you ∧?
Capitalize a letter.	/(or) ≡	*T*̸oronto (or) toronto ≡
Make a capital letter lowercase.	/	*h*H̸istory
Close up space.	⌒	ball ⌒ park
Transpose.	∩∪	America⟨s'⟩
Delete or replace.	—— (or) ϑ	*cold* a h̶o̶t̶ day (or) a n̶o̶t̶ day (or) a h̶o̶t̶ ϑ day
Insert an apostrophe or quotation marks.	∨' ∨'' ∨''	Bill ∨'s ∨''Wow! ∨''
Use italics.	_____	<u>Tracker</u>
Insert parentheses.	(∧)∧	letters (∧ from A to Z)∧

MUG Shot
OVERVIEW

This overview includes a reproducible sheet for students to organize their daily sentences. There are also implementation guidelines and a helpful catalog of the types of writing problems addressed in *Daily Language Workouts 10*.

Note: A useful guide to editing and proofreading marks is on page iv.

MUG Shot Sentence Organizer

Original Sentence:

_____

_____

Corrected Sentence:

_____

_____

Original Sentence:

_____

_____

Corrected Sentence:

_____

_____

Original Sentence:

_____

_____

Corrected Sentence:

_____

_____

Original Sentence:

_____

_____

Corrected Sentence:

_____

_____

Original Sentence:

_____

_____

Corrected Sentence:

_____

_____

Using MUG Shot Sentences and Paragraphs

Implementation

The sentences and paragraphs in this booklet provide a thorough study of the most common errors students make in mechanics, usage, and grammar. Each of the first 15 sets of sentences focuses on a particular type of problem—punctuation, capitalization, subject-verb agreement, and so on. The remaining sets provide a mixed review.

On the days that you use the MUG Shot sentences, we suggest that you write one or two of them on the board at the beginning of the class period. Allow students time to read each sentence to themselves. (Make sure they understand the sentences.) Then have students correct each sentence in a space reserved for them in their notebooks (or on a copy of the "MUG Shot Sentence Organizer" provided on page 2). Have students discuss their corrections in pairs or as a class. Make sure everyone eventually has the correct form of the sentence recorded and that all students understand why the corrections were made.

You may also have students orally correct the sentences. Write the corrections on the board as a volunteer provides them. Have the student explain his or her corrections and discuss the results. Then ask all students to write the corrected form in their notebooks.

The MUG Shot Paragraphs review the sentences covered for the week and contain errors similar to the type students worked on for the week. Each paragraph is followed by a sentence-combining activity.

Note: By design, each page of sentences can be reproduced for student use or made into a transparency.

Evaluation

If you assign sentences daily, evaluate your students' work at the end of each week. We recommend that you give students a basic performance score for their work. This score might be based on how well they did on each sentence or on simply having each sentence correctly written in their notebooks (before or after any discussion). You might also have students exchange and correct the weekly paragraph and use the results to evaluate their progress.

Important note: Because some errors—such as sentence fragments, comma splices, and run-on and rambling sentences—can be corrected in more than one way, you need to consider this when evaluating student work.

Errors Covered in the
Daily Language Workouts

Each kind of error covered in the *Daily Language Workouts* is listed below. The errors are also listed above each sentence and paragraph. Some of the more challenging errors are identified in greater detail than the others. For example, five comma errors are identified specifically, such as "Comma (To Separate Adjectives)." The more common errors are listed as "Comma (Other)."

Punctuation

- End Punctuation
- Comma (To Separate Adjectives)
- Comma (Nonrestrictive Phrase or Clause)
- Comma (Appositive)
- Comma (Unnecessary)
- Comma (Parenthetical or Contrasted Elements)
- Comma (Other) *includes*
  - Series
  - Numbers
  - Dates
  - Addresses
  - Dialogue
  - Interruptions
  - Direct Address
  - To Set Off Interjections
  - Titles or Initials
  - Between Independent Clauses
  - Introductory Phrases & Clauses
- Semicolon
- Colon
- Dash
- Parentheses
- Hyphen
- Quotation Marks *includes*
  - Misplaced
  - Direct Quotation
  - Single
  - Special Words
- Apostrophe
- Diagonal
- Brackets
- Italics (Underlining)
- Punctuation (Title) *includes*
  - Quotation Marks
  - Italics/Underlining

Mechanics

- Using the Right Word
- Capitalization
- Plurals
- Abbreviation
- Numbers
- Spelling

Parts of Speech

- Adverb Form
- Adjective Form
- Article
- Verb (Tense)
- Verb (Irregular)
- Pronoun Usage
- Pronoun (Case)

Using the Language

- Combining Sentences
- Parallel Structure
- Subject-Verb Agreement
- Pronoun-Antecedent Agreement
- Sentence Fragment
- Double Negative
- Rambling Sentence
- Comma Splice
- Run-On Sentence
- Misplaced Modifier
- Dangling Modifier
- Nonstandard Language
- Fair Language
- Indefinite Pronoun Reference
- Deadwood/Wordiness
- Shift in Construction

Daily SENTENCES
Weekly PARAGRAPHS/ SENTENCE COMBINING

Daily Sentences

The MUG Shot sentences are designed to be used at the beginning of each class period as a quick and efficient way to review mechanics, usage, and grammar. (Each MUG Shot sentence can be corrected and discussed in 3 to 5 minutes.)

Weekly Paragraphs/Sentence Combining

The MUG Shot paragraphs can be used at the end of each week as a review of the week's sentences. Each paragraph is followed by a sentence-combining activity. (The paragraph corrections and sentence-combining activity can be accomplished in 10 to 15 minutes.)

Set 1: Focus on Punctuation

@ **Comma (Unnecessary), Spelling, Comma (Other)**

Exercize, in fact, stimulates the release of endorphins, that can make people feel good but many people still prefer being couch potatoes.

@ **Comma (Unnecessary), Using the Right Word, Spelling**

In anshunt Incan society, couples were considered marryed when they took off there shoes, and handed them to each other.

@ **Comma (To Separate Adjectives), Spelling, Comma (Nonrestrictive Phrase or Clause), Apostrophe, Using the Right Word**

Elizabeth Blackwell who was a determined courageous beleiver in womens rites overcame alot of obstacals to become the first woman doctor in America.

@ **Comma (Unnecessary), Spelling, Punctuation (Title), Comma (To Separate Adjectives)**

Incidently, two of comedian, Charlie Chaplin's, finest funniest movies are City Lights (1931) and The Gold Rush (1925).

@ **Comma (Other), Apostrophe, Spelling, Run-On Sentence**

Thruout history, traveling traders and merchants took home new products, such as tea, spices and fabrics as a matter of fact thats one reason civilizations changed.

© Great Source. All rights reserved. (10)

Corrected Sentences

@ **Comma (Unnecessary), Spelling, Comma (Other)**

Exercise
~~Exercize~~, in fact, stimulates the release of endorphins/ that can make people feel good,

but many people still prefer being couch potatoes.

@ **Comma (Unnecessary), Using the Right Word, Spelling**

ancient   *married*   *their*
In ~~anshunt~~ Incan society, couples were considered ~~marryed~~ when they took off ~~there~~

shoes/ and handed them to each other.

@ **Comma (To Separate Adjectives), Spelling, Comma (Nonrestrictive Phrase or Clause), Apostrophe, Using the Right Word**

                                                     believer   's/ *rights*
Elizabeth Blackwell who was a determined, courageous ~~beleiver~~ in women's ~~rites~~,

              a lot   *obstacles*
overcame ~~alot~~ of ~~obstacals~~ to become the first woman doctor in America.

@ **Comma (Unnecessary), Spelling, Punctuation (Title), Comma (To Separate Adjectives)**

Incidentally
~~Incidently~~, two of comedian/ Charlie Chaplin's/ finest, funniest movies are City Lights

(1931) and The Gold Rush (1925).

@ **Comma (Other), Apostrophe, Spelling, Run-On Sentence**

Throughout
~~Thruout~~ history, traveling traders and merchants took home new products, such as tea,

spices, and fabrics, as a matter of fact, that's one reason civilizations changed.

First Female Doctor in United States

Comma (Nonrestrictive Phrase or Clause), Spelling, Comma (Unnecessary), Apostrophe, Using the Right Word, Comma (To Separate Adjectives), Comma (Other)

1   Elizabeth Blackwell became the first woman in the United States to recieve a

2   medical degree. She was born in 1821 in England. Rejected at 29 medical schools

3   Blackwell was accepted in 1847 at Geneva College in western New York, and

4   graduated with highest honors. Even so, she was unable to find a hospitol that

5   would except her credentials. To continue her studies she went to Europe, where

6   she contracted an eye diseaze from a baby that she was treating in a clinic for

7   the poor. Eventualy, she lost the sight in her left eye and it had to be removed.

8   Returning to New York she and her sister who also became a doctor, opened a

9   hospital for women and children. During the Civil War which was the bloodiest

10   deadliest war in Americas histry they trained nurses for the Union Army.

Sentence Combining

Combine the sentence that begins in line 1 and the first sentence that begins in line 2 using a **relative pronoun**. (See page 704 in *Write Source* for an example.) Put the less important idea in the subordinate clause. Write your combined sentence below.

_____

_____

_____

_____

Corrected Paragraph

@ Comma (Nonrestrictive Phrase or Clause), Spelling, Comma (Unnecessary), Apostrophe, Using the Right Word, Comma (To Separate Adjectives), Comma (Other)

1   Elizabeth Blackwell became the first woman in the United States to ~~recieve~~ *receive* a

2   medical degree. She was born in 1821 in England. Rejected at 29 medical schools,

3   Blackwell was accepted in 1847 at Geneva College in western New York and

4   graduated with highest honors. Even so, she was unable to find a ~~hospitol~~ *hospital* that

5   would ~~except~~ *accept* her credentials. To continue her studies, she went to Europe, where

6   she contracted an eye ~~diseaze~~ *disease* from a baby that she was treating in a clinic for

7   the poor. ~~Eventualy,~~ *Eventually* she lost the sight in her left eye, and it had to be removed.

8   Returning to New York, she and her sister, who also became a doctor, opened a

9   hospital for women and children. During the Civil War, which was the bloodiest,

10 deadliest war in America's ~~histry~~ *history*, they trained nurses for the Union Army.

@ **Sentence Combining**
Combine the sentence that begins in line 1 and the first sentence that begins in line 2 using a **relative pronoun**. (See page 704 in *Write Source* for an example.) Put the less important idea in the subordinate clause. Write your combined sentence below.

Elizabeth Blackwell, who was born in 1821 in England, became the first woman in the

United States to receive a medical degree.

_____

_____

Set 2: Focus on Punctuation

⊘ Comma (Appositive), Punctuation (Title)

According to the New York Times, Mickey Mantle legendary center fielder for the New York Yankees ranks among the leading home run hitters in baseball.

⊘ Colon, Hyphen, Spelling, Comma (Unnecessary), Article, Comma (Other)

Some of the most unusual patents ever granted include the following a parakeet diaper, a baby patting machien and a alarm clock, that squirts the sleeper in the face.

⊘ End Punctuation, Comma (Parenthetical or Contrasted Elements), Apostrophe, Article, Spelling, Using the Right Word

Alaska nicknamed Sewards Folly by those who thought buying it was foolish was purchested from Russia for about two sents a acre What a bargin.

⊘ Spelling, Colon, Hyphen, Comma (Other)

These good tempered dogs are most commonly used as guyde dogs German shepherds golden retrievers and Labrador retrievers.

⊘ Comma (Appositive), Article, Comma (Unnecessary), Punctuation (Title)

Pocahontas a Disney movie is about an Native American princess who saved the life of colonist, John Smith, in the 1600s.

Corrected Sentences

@ **Comma (Appositive), Punctuation (Title)**

According to the <u>New York Times</u>, Mickey Mantle͵legendary center fielder for the New

York Yankees͵ranks among the leading home run hitters in baseball.

@ **Colon, Hyphen, Spelling, Comma (Unnecessary), Article, Comma (Other)**

Some of the most unusual patents ever granted include the following͵a parakeet

diaper, a baby͵patting *machine* ~~machien~~͵and *an* ~~a~~ alarm clock͵that squirts the sleeper in the face.

@ **End Punctuation, Comma (Parenthetical or Contrasted Elements), Apostrophe, Article, Spelling, Using the Right Word**

Alaska͵nicknamed Seward's Folly by those who thought buying it was foolish͵was

purchased ~~purchested~~ from Russia for about two *cents an* ~~sents a~~ acre.What a ~~bargin~~ *bargain*!

@ **Spelling, Colon, Hyphen, Comma (Other)**

These good͵tempered dogs are most commonly used as *guide* ~~guyde~~ dogs͵German shepherds͵

golden retrievers͵and Labrador retrievers.

@ **Comma (Appositive), Article, Comma (Unnecessary), Punctuation (Title)**

<u>Pocahontas</u>͵a Disney movie͵is about *a* ~~an~~ Native American princess who saved the life

of colonist͵John Smith͵in the 1600s.

Dogs That See for People Who Don't

@ Comma (Appositive), Colon, Comma (Other), Hyphen, Italics (Underlining), Apostrophe, Spelling, Using the Right Word

1   Schools to train gide dogs began after World War I. The first American

2 gide-dog school The Seeing Eye, Inc. began in 1929. The most popular guide dogs are

3 these German shepherds golden retrievers and Labrador retrievers. Gide dogs learn

4 to lead the blind across streets and around obstacles wholes low hanging awnings

5 or tree limbs. The dogs must also exercise good judgment. For example if a blind

6 person gives a command to walk and the guide dog sees danger, the dog must

7 disobey. This is called 'intelligent disobediance.' Guide-dog schools are fairly recent.

8 Paintings scrolls and legends tell of dogs faithfull service since at least 100 B.C.E.

@ Sentence Combining
Combine the second sentence that begins in line 7 and the sentence that begins in line 8 using an **introductory clause**. (See page 610.3 in *Write Source* for an example.) Write your combined sentence below.

_____

_____

_____

_____

Corrected Paragraph

℮ Comma (Appositive), Colon, Comma (Other), Hyphen, Italics (Underlining), Apostrophe, Spelling, Using the Right Word

1   Schools to train *guide* ~~gide~~ dogs began after World War I. The first American

2   *guide* ~~gide~~-dog school, The Seeing Eye, Inc., began in 1929. The most popular guide dogs are

3   these: German shepherds, golden retrievers, and Labrador retrievers. *Guide* ~~Gide~~ dogs learn

4   to lead the blind across streets and around obstacles: *holes* ~~wholes~~, low-hanging awnings,

5   or tree limbs. The dogs must also exercise good judgment. For example, if a blind

6   person gives a command to walk and the guide dog sees danger, the dog must

7   disobey. This is called "intelligent *disobedience* ~~disobediance~~." Guide-dog schools are fairly recent.

8   Paintings, scrolls, and legends tell of dogs' *faithful* ~~faithfull~~ service since at least 100 B.C.E.

℮ Sentence Combining
Combine the second sentence that begins in line 7 and the sentence that begins in line 8 using an **introductory clause**. (See page 610.3 in *Write Source* for an example.) Write your combined sentence below.

Though guide-dog schools are fairly recent, paintings, scrolls, and legends tell of

dogs' faithful service since at least 100 B.C.E.

Writers INC p. 95

Set 3: Focus on Punctuation

Quotation Marks, Comma (Other), Hyphen, Apostrophe, End Punctuation

When asked if life is worth living, did Charles great grandmother really say Well it depends upon the liver.

Quotation Marks, Comma (Other), Punctuation (Title)

General Colin Powell was quoted in the August 21 1995 issue of U.S. News and World Report as saying "We should sacrifice for one another care about one another never be satisfied when anybody in this group is suffering and we can do something about it".

Comma (Other), Dash, Numbers

Animals, plants, fungi, protists and monerans these are the 5 groups into which all living things are divided.

Comma (Appositive), Spelling, Capitalization

Bricks, the oldest building materiol on earth, were probly invented in egypt home of the pyramids.

Dash, Comma (Nonrestrictive Phrase or Clause), Hyphen, Apostrophe, Comma (Other)

My sister in law who is a 4-H leader explained, "Head, heart, hands and health these are what the four Hs in 4-H stand for."

Corrected Sentences

❷ Quotation Marks, Comma (Other), Hyphen, Apostrophe, End Punctuation

When asked if life is worth living, did Charles' *(or)* 's great-grandmother really say, "Well, it depends upon the liver"?

❷ Quotation Marks, Comma (Other), Punctuation (Title)

General Colin Powell was quoted in the August 21, 1995, issue of U.S. News and World Report as saying, "We should sacrifice for one another, care about one another, never be satisfied when anybody in this group is suffering and we can do something about it."

❷ Comma (Other), Dash, Numbers

Animals, plants, fungi, protists, and monerans—these are the *five* 5 groups into which all living things are divided.

❷ Comma (Appositive), Spelling, Capitalization

Bricks, the oldest building *material* materiol on earth, were *probably* probly invented in *E*gypt, home of the pyramids.

❷ Dash, Comma (Nonrestrictive Phrase or Clause), Hyphen, Apostrophe, Comma (Other)

My sister-in-law, who is a 4-H leader, explained, "Head, heart, hands, and health—these are what the four H's in 4-H stand for."

Bricks Bridge Time

ℯ Comma (Parenthetical or Contrasted Elements), Quotation Marks, Comma (Unnecessary), Indefinite Pronoun Reference, Spelling, Hyphen, Comma (Other), Dash, Using the Right Word, Capitalization

1   They may be the oldest building material on earth and were probly

2   descoverd by accident. The Empire State Building has over 10 million bricks. The

3   Great Wall of China has almost 4 billion. My brother in law, a bricklayer, says

4   'brick building is not for everyone.' Homes factories roads all of these can be built

5   of brick but the first bricks were probably formed when somebody along a river

6   such as the Nile River in Egypt picked up some mud, formed it into a shape left

7   it out in the sun and than realised that it could be used for building. The oldest

8   sun dried brick ever found is from beneath the biblical city of Jericho, and is

9   about 10,000 years old.

ℯ **Sentence Combining**
Combine the sentences that begin in line 2 using a **coordinating conjunction**. (See page 734.1 in *Write Source* for an example.) Write your combined sentence below.

_____

_____

_____

_____

Corrected Paragraph

⊘ Comma (Parenthetical or Contrasted Elements), Quotation Marks, Comma (Unnecessary),
Indefinite Pronoun Reference, Spelling, Hyphen, Comma (Other), Dash, Using the Right Word,
Capitalization

1   *Bricks*
     ~~They~~ may be the oldest building material on earth and were ~~probly~~ *probably*

2   *discovered*
     ~~descovered~~ by accident. The Empire State Building has over 10 million bricks. The

3   Great Wall of China has almost 4 billion. My brother-in-law, a bricklayer, says,

4   "*B*rick building is not for everyone." Homes, factories, roads—all of these can be built

5   of brick, but the first bricks were probably formed when somebody along a river,

6   such as the Nile River in Egypt, picked up some mud, formed it into a shape, left

7   it out in the sun, and ~~than~~ *then* ~~realised~~ *realized* that it could be used for building. The oldest

8   sun-dried brick ever found is from beneath the biblical city of Jericho, and is

9   about 10,000 years old.

⊘ **Sentence Combining**
Combine the sentences that begin in line 2 using a **coordinating conjunction**. (See
page 734.1 in *Write Source* for an example.) Write your combined sentence below.

The Empire State Building has over 10 million bricks, and the Great Wall of China

has almost 4 billion.

_____

_____

Set 4: Focus on Capitalization and Sentence Fragments

@ **Capitalization, Sentence Fragment, Nonstandard Language, Comma (Appositive)**

Manhattan island the smallest County in the United States. It is also the most populous. (ain't that something?)

@ **Capitalization, Sentence Fragment, Italics (Underlining), Using the Right Word, Spelling**

My Uncle learned me that "the t in the expression fit to a tee comes from the T-square." A tool Carpenters use to make sure measurments are acurate.

@ **Capitalization, Sentence Fragment, Comma (Other), Colon**

The state of Texas has had the following six National flags flying over it. Spain France Mexico the republic of Texas the confederate states of America and the United States of America.

@ **Capitalization, Sentence Fragment, Spelling**

One of the intresting tidbits we learned in History class (My favorite subject). Is that jeans are a by-product of the gold rush of 1849.

@ **Comma (Parenthetical or Contrasted Elements), Using the Right Word, Comma (Other), Capitalization, Comma (Unnecessary)**

George Washington Carver, born a slave during the civil war introduced crop rotation to poor farmers in the rural south, and discovered alot of uses for peanuts, soybeans and sweet potatoes.

Corrected Sentences

Capitalization, Sentence Fragment, Nonstandard Language, Comma (Appositive)

Manhattan ~~i~~**I**sland, the smallest ~~c~~**C**ounty in the United States, ~~It~~ is also the most populous. (~~ain't~~ **Isn't** that something?)

Capitalization, Sentence Fragment, Italics (Underlining), Using the Right Word, Spelling

My ~~u~~**U**ncle ~~learned~~ **taught** me that the <u>t</u> in the expression <u>fit to a tee</u> comes from the T-square, ~~a~~**A** tool ~~c~~**C**arpenters use to make sure ~~measurments~~ **measurements** are ~~acurate~~ **accurate**.

Capitalization, Sentence Fragment, Comma (Other), Colon

The state of Texas has had the following six ~~N~~ational flags flying over it: Spain, France, Mexico, the ~~r~~**R**epublic of Texas, the ~~c~~**C**onfederate ~~s~~**S**tates of America, and the United States of America.

Capitalization, Sentence Fragment, Spelling

One of the ~~intresting~~ **interesting** tidbits we learned in ~~h~~**H**istory class (~~M~~**M**y favorite subject) ~~i~~**I**s that jeans are a by-product of the gold rush of 1849.

Comma (Parenthetical or Contrasted Elements), Using the Right Word, Comma (Other), Capitalization, Comma (Unnecessary)

George Washington Carver, born a slave during the ~~c~~**C**ivil ~~w~~**W**ar, introduced crop rotation to poor farmers in the rural ~~s~~**S**outh, and discovered ~~alot~~ **a lot** of uses for peanuts, soybeans, and sweet potatoes.

Jeans for Prospectors

@ Capitalization, Sentence Fragments, Quotation Marks, Comma (Appositive), Comma (Other), Plurals, Comma (Unnecessary), Abbreviation

1   The california Gold Rush of 1849 attracted thousands of prospectors. 'Go west

2   young man' was the cry. Levi Straus left new york in 1850. He went west to san

3   francisco where he planned to sell canvas, for tents and Conestoga wagon covers

4   to the prospectors. He soon realized that hardworking prospector's needed sturdy

5   work pants. Levi had a Tailor make some pants from brown canvas. Soon many

6   prospectors were wearing durable work pants. When the canvas was gone. Levi

7   switched to Denim another sturdy fabric. Today, when you pull on a pair of jeans,

8   say thank-you to mister levi straus.

@ **Sentence Combining**
Combine the sentences that begin in line 2 using a **relative pronoun**. (See page 706.2 in *Write Source* for an example.) Write your combined sentence below.

_____

_____

_____

_____

Corrected Paragraph

℮ Capitalization, Sentence Fragments, Quotation Marks, Comma (Appositive), Comma (Other), Plurals, Comma (Unnecessary), Abbreviation

1   The california Gold Rush of 1849 attracted thousands of prospectors. Go west,

2 young man was the cry. Levi Straus left new york in 1850. He went west to san

3 francisco where he planned to sell canvas for tents and Conestoga wagon covers

4 to the prospectors. He soon realized that hardworking prospectors needed sturdy

5 work pants. Levi had a Tailor make some pants from brown canvas. Soon many

6 prospectors were wearing durable work pants. When the canvas was gone, Levi

7 switched to Denim, another sturdy fabric. Today, when you pull on a pair of jeans,

8 say thank-you to ~~mister~~ Mr. Levi straus.

℮ Sentence Combining

Combine the sentences that begin in line 2 using a **relative pronoun**. (See page 706.2 in *Write Source* for an example.) Write your combined sentence below.

Levi Strauss, who left New York in 1850, went west to San Francisco where he

planned to sell canvas for tents and Conestoga wagon covers to the prospectors.

Set 5: Focus on Capitalization and Comma Splices

@ Capitalization, Comma Splice, Parentheses

In the 1905 Football Season, 18 players were killed, president Theodore Roosevelt established the national collegiate athletic association ncaa to make the game safer.

@ Capitalization, Comma Splice, Spelling, Italics (Underlining)

The book of genesis, which is honored by jews, muslims, and christians alike, contains a detailed discription of Noah's Ark, the battleship Oregon was built to the same meashurements.

@ Capitalization, Comma Splice, Using the Right Word, Abbreviation

South Dakota is the geographical center of the United States, its also the home of mt. rushmore, the mountain that has the likenesses of four U.S. Presidents carved into it.

@ Capitalization, Comma (Nonrestrictive Phrase or Clause), Quotation Marks, Comma (Other), Spelling

Whenever aunt Corrie who lives in the western suburbs of Chicago gets asked how to get to lake Michigan, she says drive straight East untill you fall in.

@ Punctuation (Title), Capitalization, Comma Splice, Hyphen

The song the daring young man on the flying trapeze was written about Jules Léotard, a french trapeze artist, his second claim to fame was the tight fitting garment that was named after him.

Corrected Sentences

◉ **Capitalization, Comma Splice, Parentheses**

In the 1905 ~~f~~F**ootball** ~~s~~S**eason**, 18 players were killed, **so** **P**resident Theodore Roosevelt established the **N**ational **C**ollegiate **A**thletic **A**ssociation **(NCAA)** ~~ncaa~~ to make the game safer.

◉ **Capitalization, Comma Splice, Spelling, Italics (Underlining)**

The **B**ook of **G**enesis, which is honored by **J**ews, **M**uslims, and **C**hristians alike, contains a detailed *description* ~~discription~~ of Noah's Ark**; a** the battleship <u>Oregon</u> was built to the same *measurements* ~~meashurements~~.

◉ **Capitalization, Comma Splice, Using the Right Word, Abbreviation**

South Dakota is the geographical center of the United States**; It's** ~~its~~ also the home of **M**t. **R**ushmore, the mountain that has the likenesses of four ~~U.S.~~ *United States* **P**residents carved into it.

◉ **Capitalization, Comma (Nonrestrictive Phrase or Clause), Quotation Marks, Comma (Other), Spelling**

Whenever **A**unt Corrie**,** who lives in the western suburbs of Chicago**,** gets asked how to get to **L**ake Michigan, she says**," D**rive straight **E**ast *until* ~~untill~~ you fall in**."**

◉ **Punctuation (Title), Capitalization, Comma Splice, Hyphen**

The song **"**The **D**aring **Y**oung **M**an on the **F**lying **T**rapeze**"** was written about Jules Léotard, a **F**rench trapeze artist**; H**is second claim to fame was the tight-fitting garment that was named after him.

Football Facts

℮ Comma Splice, Capitalization, Spelling, Punctuation (Title), Comma (Appositive), Abbreviation, Comma (Other)

1　　　According to Gail b Slap, md and Martha M Jablow authors of the book

2　teenage health care, over 80 percent of high school athleats who play football are

3　out with injuries for at least four days of the season. Ancient romans played a

4　game similar to modern football using an inflated animal bladder, they introduced

5　the game to the british isles which they conquered around 100 BCE. The first

6　paid player was William Heffelfinger, he played for the allegheny athletic

7　association on november 12 1892 and was paid $500. The information please

8　almanac says that the first professional football game in the united states was

9　played in 1895 in latrobe pennsylvania. The national football league (nfl) wasn't

10　founded until 1921.

℮ Sentence Combining
Combine the sentences that begin in lines 7 and 9 using a **semicolon** and a **conjunctive adverb**. (See page 618.2 in *Write Source* for an example; also see 618.2 for a list of conjunctive adverbs.) Write your combined sentence below.

_____

_____

_____

_____

Corrected Paragraph

Comma Splice, Capitalization, Spelling, Punctuation (Title), Comma (Appositive), Abbreviation, Comma (Other)

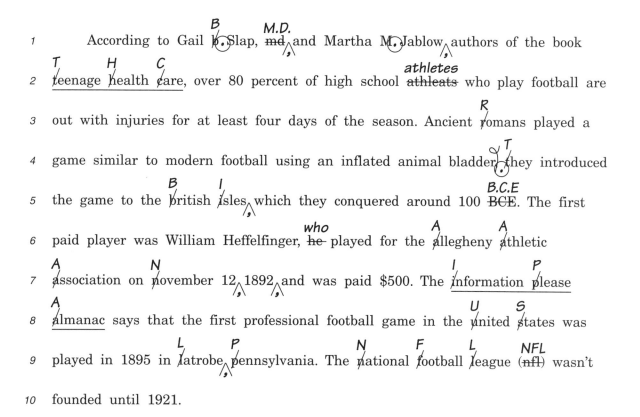

1   According to Gail B. Slap, M.D. and Martha M. Jablow, authors of the book

2   teenage health care, over 80 percent of high school athletes who play football are

3   out with injuries for at least four days of the season. Ancient Romans played a

4   game similar to modern football using an inflated animal bladder. They introduced

5   the game to the British Isles, which they conquered around 100 B.C.E. The first

6   paid player was William Heffelfinger, who played for the Allegheny Athletic

7   Association on November 12, 1892, and was paid $500. The Information Please

8   Almanac says that the first professional football game in the United States was

9   played in 1895 in Latrobe, Pennsylvania. The National Football League (NFL) wasn't

10 founded until 1921.

Sentence Combining

Combine the sentences that begin in lines 7 and 9 using a **semicolon** and a **conjunctive adverb**. (See page 618.2 in *Write Source* for an example; also see 618.2 for a list of conjunctive adverbs.) Write your combined sentence below.

The Information Please Almanac says that the first professional football game

in the United States was played in 1895 in Latrobe, Pennsylvania; however, the

National Football League (NFL) wasn't founded until 1921.

Set 6: Focus on Plurals, Numbers, and Abbreviations

@ Numbers, Comma (Unnecessary), Comma Splice, Using the Right Word, Abbreviation

They're more than 1,000,000 different kinds of insects in the world, they comprise 78% of all creatures, and together weigh twelve times more than the combined weight of all humans.

@ Plurals, Numbers, Abbreviation, Run-On Sentence, Using the Right Word

In crisis that involve injurys too muscles and ligaments, remember the acronym Rice the 4 letters stand four rest, ice, compression, and elevation.

@ Numbers, Comma (Other), Abbreviation

$5,000 was the amount the great racing horse Man O' War was sold for in 1918 but he and his three hundred eighty-three descendants earned close to 6,000,000 dollars.

@ Plurals, Comma, Using the Right Word

Under three rooves three attornies in three studioes made three wishs jumped into three jalopys, stuck there heads out of three windows and decided between themselves where to go for lunch.

@ Abbreviation, Comma (Other), Using the Right Word, Spelling

If you're snoring is a problem get help and information by sending a bizness-sized s.a.s.e. (self-addressed stamped envelope) to the following address: N. York Eye & Ear Infirmary Second Ave. at 14th St. N.Y., N.Y. 10003.

Corrected Sentences

Numbers, Comma (Unnecessary), Comma Splice, Using the Right Word, Abbreviation

There are ~~They're~~ more than *1 million* ~~1,000,000~~ different kinds of insects in the world; *T*hey comprise *percent* ~~78%~~ of all creatures, and together weigh *12* ~~twelve~~ times more than the combined weight of all humans.

Plurals, Numbers, Abbreviation, Run-On Sentence, Using the Right Word

In *crises* ~~crisis~~ that involve *injuries to* ~~injurys too~~ muscles and ligaments, remember the acronym *RICE* ~~Rice~~; the *four* ~~4~~ letters stand *for* ~~four~~ rest, ice, compression, and elevation.

Numbers, Comma (Other), Abbreviation

Five thousand dollars ~~$5,000~~ was the amount the great racing horse Man O' War was sold for in 1918, but he and his *383* ~~three hundred eighty-three~~ descendants earned close to *$6 million* ~~6,000,000 dollars~~.

Plurals, Comma, Using the Right Word

Under three *roofs* ~~rooves~~ three *attorneys* ~~attornies~~ in three *studios* ~~studioes~~ made three *wishes* ~~wishs~~, jumped into three *jalopies* ~~jalopys~~, stuck *their* ~~there~~ heads out of three windows, and decided *among* ~~between~~ themselves where to go for lunch.

Abbreviation, Comma (Other), Using the Right Word, Spelling

If *your* ~~you're~~ snoring is a problem, get help and information by sending a *business* ~~bizness~~-sized *SASE* ~~s.a.s.e.~~ (self-addressed stamped envelope) to the following address: *New* ~~N.~~ York Eye & Ear Infirmary, Second *Avenue* ~~Ave.~~ at 14th *Street* ~~St.~~, *New York, New York* ~~N.Y., N.Y.~~ 10003.

Millionaire Horse

Plurals, Numbers, Abbreviation, Comma (Nonrestrictive Phrase or Clause), Capitalization, Spelling, Comma (Other), Using the Right Word

1   Horse racing has thrived in this country since the Amer. revolution, and

2   thoroughbred horses can all be traced back to 3 sires brought to Eng. from the

3   near east around 1728. 1 of the descendants of these thoroughbreds was Man O'

4   War who in a 2-year carear won twenty out of the 21 races (95%) that he entered.

5   Bought for five thousand dollars at auction in 1918, Man O' War earned close to

6    $2,000,000 in winnings and stud fees. He sired three hundred eighty-three son's

7   and daughter's who's combined earnings were close to $4,000,000. When Man O'

8   War died on Nov. 1 1947 his obit. was printed in the major newspapers. 2,500

9   admirers attended his funeral.

Sentence Combining
Combine the sentences that begin in lines 7 and 8 using a **semicolon**. (See page 618.1 in *Write Source* for an example.) Write your combined sentence below.

_____

_____

_____

_____

Corrected Paragraph

@ **Plurals, Numbers, Abbreviation, Comma (Nonrestrictive Phrase or Clause), Capitalization, Spelling, Comma (Other), Using the Right Word**

1   Horse racing has thrived in this country since the ~~Amer.~~ *AmericanR*/evolution, and

2   thoroughbred horses can all be traced back to ~~3~~ *three* sires brought to ~~Eng.~~ *England* from the

3   /*N*ear /*E*ast around 1728. ~~1~~ *One* of the descendants of these thoroughbreds was Man O'

4   War,/ who in a ~~2~~*two*-year ~~carear~~ *career* won ~~twenty~~ *20* out of the 21 races (95% *percent*) that he entered.

5   Bought for ~~five thousand dollars~~ *$5,000* at auction in 1918, Man O' War earned close to

6   ~~$2,000,000~~ *$2 million* in winnings and stud fees. He sired ~~three hundred eighty-three~~ *383* son's

7   and daughter's ~~who's~~ *whose* combined earnings were close to ~~$4,000,000~~ *$4 million*. When Man O'

8   War died on ~~Nov.~~ *November* 1,/ 1947,/ his ~~obit.~~ *obituary* was printed in the major newspapers. ~~2,500~~ *Twenty-five hundred*

9   admirers attended his funeral.

@ **Sentence Combining**

Combine the sentences that begin in lines 7 and 8 using a **semicolon**. (See page 618.1 in *Write Source* for an example.) Write your combined sentence below.

When Man O' War died on November 1, 1947, his obituary was printed in the major

newspapers; 2,500 admirers attended his funeral.

Set 7: Focus on Rambling and Run-On Sentences

☉ Rambling Sentence, Using the Right Word

Knuckles crack because when you pull apart the too bones in fingers or toes, a fluid slips into the space and this action causes a low-pressure condition, and bubbles form and then collapse.

☉ Run-On Sentence, Numbers, Using the Right Word, Abbreviation

75% of all people have at least one cold a year while 25% have four or more teenagers are fifty % more likely to catch cold then people over fifty are.

☉ Run-On Sentence, Comma (Other), Numbers, Apostrophe

An elephants' trunk has forty thousand muscles that can be used for feeding digging bathing locating food or smelling danger the trunk can uproot a tree or pick up a pin.

☉ Rambling Sentence, Comma (Other), Numbers

A terrible hurricane hit New England and Long Island, New York, in September 1938 and 600 people were killed and 275,000,000 trees were destroyed and 20,000 miles of electric wires were downed and 26,000 cars were damaged.

☉ Numbers, Punctuation (Title), Comma (Unnecessary)

In his book, Les Misérables, French author Victor Hugo wrote a sentence that has eight hundred twenty-three words, ninety-three commas, fifty-one semicolons, and four dashes.

Corrected Sentences

⊘ Rambling Sentence, Using the Right Word

Knuckles crack because when you pull apart the ~~too~~ *two* bones in fingers or toes, a fluid slips into the space. ~~and~~ *T*his action causes a low-pressure condition, and bubbles form and then collapse.

⊘ Run-On Sentence, Numbers, Using the Right Word, Abbreviation

Seventy-five percent ~~75%~~ of all people have at least one cold a year while 25% *percent* have four or more. *T*eenagers are ~~fifty %~~ *50 percent* more likely to catch cold ~~then~~ *than* people over ~~fifty~~ *50* are.

⊘ Run-On Sentence, Comma (Other), Numbers, Apostrophe

An elephant's trunk has ~~forty thousand~~ *40,000* muscles that can be used for feeding, digging, bathing, locating food, or smelling danger; the trunk can uproot a tree or pick up a pin.

⊘ Rambling Sentence, Comma (Other), Numbers

A terrible hurricane hit New England and Long Island, New York, in September 1938; ~~and~~ 600 people were killed, and ~~275,000,000~~ *275 million* trees were destroyed, and 20,000 miles of electric wires were downed, and 26,000 cars were damaged.

⊘ Numbers, Punctuation (Title), Comma (Unnecessary)

In his book, Les Misérables, French author Victor Hugo wrote a sentence that has ~~eight hundred twenty-three~~ *823* words, ~~ninety-three~~ *93* commas, ~~fifty-one~~ *51* semicolons, and ~~four~~ *4* dashes.

Common Sense and the Common Cold

Writers INC p. 548.1

⊚ Rambling Sentence, Run-On Sentence, Numbers, Using the Right Word, Comma (Other), Spelling, Capitalization, Apostrophe, Hyphen

1   Scientists and Researchers dont seem a whole lot closer now than they were

2   100 years ago to curing the Common Cold and it will run it's course in seven to

3   10 days whether or not you treat it and antibiotics do no good because colds are

4   caused by viruses and antibiotics cant kill viruses. Over the counter medications

5   can make you feel better but they won't cure a cold either extra rest (lay off the

6   parties!) and lots of clear lickwids help and scientists have verified that there is

7   actualy something in chicken soup that unclogs your nasal passages. I love the

8   books that tell you to seek medical help if anything green and bloody comes out of

9   you're nose. The books also say to seek medical help if you lose consciousness.

⊚ **Sentence Combining**
Combine the sentences that begin in lines 7 and 9 using a **coordinating conjunction**. (See page 734 in *Write Source* for an example and a list of coordinating conjunctions.)
Write your combined sentence below.

_____

_____

_____

_____

Corrected Paragraph

@ **Rambling Sentence, Run-On Sentence, Numbers, Using the Right Word, Comma (Other), Spelling, Capitalization, Apostrophe, Hyphen**

1   Scientists and Researchers don't seem a whole lot closer now than they were

2   100 years ago to curing the Common Cold. and it will run it's course in seven to

3   10 days whether or not you treat it. and antibiotics do no good because colds are

4   caused by viruses, and antibiotics can't kill viruses. Over the counter medications

5   can make you feel better, but they won't cure a cold either, extra rest (lay off the

6   parties!) and lots of clear lickwids help. and scientists have verified that there is

7   actually something in chicken soup that unclogs your nasal passages. I love the

8   books that tell you to seek medical help if anything green and bloody comes out of

9   you're nose. The books also say to seek medical help if you lose consciousness.

@ **Sentence Combining**

Combine the sentences that begin in lines 7 and 9 using a **coordinating conjunction**. (See page 734 in *Write Source* for an example and a list of coordinating conjunctions.) Write your combined sentence below.

I love the books that tell you to seek medical help if anything green and bloody

comes out of your nose or if you lose consciousness.

Set 8: Focus on Pronoun Problems

@ **Pronoun-Antecedent Agreement, Pronoun (Case), Comma Splice, Using the Right Word**

Each student needs their own computer to practice on, its a shame that the supply ran out before Mr. Hudgens could assign a computer to Carrie and I.

@ **Pronoun-Antecedent Agreement, Spelling, Plurals**

In some countrys, makeup can idenify which tribe or religion people belong to and what rank you have within a group.

@ **Pronoun-Antecedent Agreement, Comma (Other), Abbreviation**

Mosquitoes are not a problem in cool weather because when the temperature drops below 60° it can't flap its wings.

@ **Pronoun (Case), Using the Right Word, Run-On Sentence**

Armando and me are not you're classic game geeks him and me just like to keep up with the latest trends in video games.

@ **Pronoun-Antecedent Agreement, Using the Right Word, Spelling**

Who's problem is it when a major defence corporation loses their goverment contract and lays off most of their employees?

Corrected Sentences

@ Pronoun-Antecedent Agreement, Pronoun (Case), Comma Splice, Using the Right Word

his or her   *It's*
Each student needs ~~their~~ own computer to practice on. ~~its~~ a shame that the supply

me
ran out before Mr. Hudgens could assign a computer to Carrie and ~~I~~.

@ Pronoun-Antecedent Agreement, Spelling, Plurals

countries   *identify*
In some ~~countrys~~, makeup can ~~idenify~~ which tribe or religion people belong to and

they
what rank ~~you~~ have within a group.

@ Pronoun-Antecedent Agreement, Comma (Other), Abbreviation

Mosquitoes are not a problem in cool weather because when the temperature drops

degrees they   *their*
below 60°, ~~it~~ can't flap ~~its~~ wings.

@ Pronoun (Case), Using the Right Word, Run-On Sentence

I   *your*   *he*   *I*
Armando and ~~me~~ are not ~~you're~~ classic game geeks; ~~him~~ and ~~me~~ just like to keep up

with the latest trends in video games.

@ Pronoun-Antecedent Agreement, Using the Right Word, Spelling

Whose   *defense*   *its government*
~~Who's~~ problem is it when a major ~~defence~~ corporation loses ~~their~~ ~~goverment~~ contract

its
and lays off most of ~~their~~ employees?

Let's Make Up

Pronoun-Antecedent Agreement, Using the Right Word, Sentence Fragment, Hyphen, Spelling, Apostrophe, Comma Splice, Comma (Other), Dash or Parentheses

1   People all around the world pay alot of attention to makeup. They like to

2   look good. Makeup can identify which tribe or religion someone belongs to, it can

3   also show others what your rank and importance are. Or be worn for self

4   improvement. In Japan, female entertainers may wear traditional chalk white

5   makeup. A dot of red on a boys' forehead in India shows the caste (or class) they

6   belongs to, in some African tribes orange makeup symbolizes strenth and shows

7   that the person usually a man wearing it is a canadate for cheif. Dark paint on a

8   Colombian woman shows whether they is married or single. American women often

9   ware makeup to make herself look more "natural."

@ Sentence Combining
Combine the sentences that begin in line 1 using a **subordinating conjunction**. (See page 734.3 in *Write Source* for an example; also see 734.3 for a list of subordinating conjunctions.) Write your combined sentence below.

_____

_____

_____

_____

Corrected Paragraph

@ **Pronoun-Antecedent Agreement, Using the Right Word, Sentence Fragment, Hyphen, Spelling, Apostrophe, Comma Splice, Comma (Other), Dash or Parentheses**

1   People all around the world pay *a lot* ~~alot~~ of attention to makeup. They like to

2   look good. Makeup can identify which tribe or religion someone belongs to, it can

3   also show others what *someone's* ~~your~~ rank and importance are *o* ~~O~~r be worn for self-

4   improvement. In Japan, female entertainers may wear traditional chalk-white

5   makeup. A dot of red on a boy's forehead in India shows the caste (or class) *he* ~~they~~

6   belongs to. In some African tribes, orange makeup symbolizes *strength* ~~strenth~~ and shows

7   that the person —(or)(usually a man —(or)) wearing it is a *candidate* ~~canadate~~ for *chief* ~~cheif~~. Dark paint on a

8   Colombian woman shows whether *she* ~~they~~ is married or single. American women often

9   *wear* ~~ware~~ makeup to make *themselves* ~~herself~~ look more "natural."

@ **Sentence Combining**

Combine the sentences that begin in line 1 using a **subordinating conjunction**. (See page 734.3 in *Write Source* for an example; also see 734.3 for a list of subordinating conjunctions.) Write your combined sentence below.

People all around the world pay a lot of attention to makeup because they like to

look good.

Set 9: Focus on Pronoun Problems

@ **Indefinite Pronoun Reference, Comma (Other), Run-On Sentence, Spelling**

To attract customers merchants ocasionly pose live models next to mannequins they can't talk, smile, twitch or move a muscle.

@ **Indefinite Pronoun Reference, Italics (Underlining)**

He remembered the word silhouette while cutting a shape from the black paper and began to wonder where it came from.

@ **Indefinite Pronoun Reference, Pronoun Usage, Capitalization, Punctuation (Title)**

In the book Once upon a time when we were Colored, he describes hisself growing up as an african american in Mississippi during the 1950s.

[The author of this book is Clifton Taulbert.]

@ **Indefinite Pronoun Reference, Pronoun (Case), Capitalization**

As Sonja and myself loaded new software onto her computer, it made a grinding noise that reminded her and I of when we accidentally tried to run a spoon through Mother's garbage disposal.

@ **Indefinite Pronoun Reference, Spelling, Comma (Other)**

As the train rounded the dangerous curve on a specially dezigned rail it tipped inward slightly but remained stable.

Corrected Sentences

@ **Indefinite Pronoun Reference, Comma (Other), Run-On Sentence, Spelling**

To attract customers~,~ merchants ~ocasionly~ *occasionally* pose live models next to mannequins~;~ ~they~ *the models*

can't talk, smile, twitch~,~ or move a muscle.

@ **Indefinite Pronoun Reference, Italics (Underlining)**

He remembered the word <u>silhouette</u> while cutting a shape from the black paper and

began to wonder where ~it~ *the word* came from.

@ **Indefinite Pronoun Reference, Pronoun Usage, Capitalization, Punctuation (Title)**

In the book <u>Once *U*pon a *T*ime *W*hen *W*e *W*ere Colored,</u> ~he~ *Clifton Taulbert* describes ~hisself~ *himself* growing up

as an *A*frican *A*merican in Mississippi during the 1950s.

[The author of this book is Clifton Taulbert.]

@ **Indefinite Pronoun Reference, Pronoun (Case), Capitalization**

As Sonja and ~myself~ *I* loaded new software onto her computer, ~it~ *the computer* made a grinding

noise that reminded her and ~I~ *me* of when we accidentally tried to run a spoon through

m~M~other's garbage disposal.

@ **Indefinite Pronoun Reference, Spelling, Comma (Other)**

As the train rounded the dangerous curve on a specially ~dezigned~ *designed* rail~,~ ~it~ *the train* tipped inward

slightly but remained stable.

Where Do Silhouettes Come From?

🌀 Pronoun (Case), Pronoun-Antecedent Agreement, Indefinite Pronoun Reference, Abbreviation, Comma (Other), Verb (Irregular), Comma (Unnecessary), Italics (Underlining), Capitalization, Comma (Appositive)

1   My brother and me were in 1st grade at Barnes elementary school. We

2   cutted black outlines of our adorable, childlike profiles, pasted it on white sheets of

3   paper and proudly took it home to our Mom and Dad. The word silhouette comes

4   from Etienne de Silhouette the minister of finance in France in 1759. Silhouette

5   tried to place new taxes on the rich, and initiate a cutback in expenses for the

6   royal family, who were not known for his thrifty ways. This did not make

7   Silhouette popular in some circles and he was soon forced out of office. As a

8   hobby Silhouette made shadow portraits. People liked them but they were often

9   considered art *on the cheap*, and they became known as *silhouettes*.

🌀 **Sentence Combining**
Combine the sentences that begin in line 1 using an **introductory clause**. (See page 610.3 in *Write Source* for an example.) Write your combined sentence below.

_____

_____

_____

_____

Corrected Paragraph

 Pronoun (Case), Pronoun-Antecedent Agreement, Indefinite Pronoun Reference, Abbreviation, Comma (Other), Verb (Irregular), Comma (Unnecessary), Italics (Underlining), Capitalization, Comma (Appositive)

1   My brother and ~~me~~ *I* were in ~~1st~~ *first* grade at Barnes ~~e~~*E*lementary ~~s~~*S*chool. We

2 ~~cutted~~ *cut* black outlines of our adorable, childlike profiles, pasted ~~it~~ *them* on white sheets of

3 paper *,* and proudly took ~~it~~ *them* home to our ~~M~~*m*om and ~~D~~*d*ad. The word silhouette comes

4 from Etienne de Silhouette *,* the minister of finance in France in 1759. Silhouette

5 tried to place new taxes on the rich *,* and initiate a cutback in expenses for the

6 royal family, who were not known for ~~his~~ *their* thrifty ways. This did not make

7 Silhouette popular in some circles *,* and he was soon forced out of office. As a

8 hobby *,* Silhouette made shadow portraits. People liked them *,* but ~~they~~ *the portraits* were often

9 considered art "on the cheap," and they became known as "silhouettes."

Sentence Combining
Combine the sentences that begin in line 1 using an **introductory clause**. (See page 610.3 in *Write Source* for an example.) Write your combined sentence below.

When my brother and I were in first grade at Barnes Elementary School, we cut

black outlines of our adorable, childlike profiles, pasted them on white sheets of

paper, and proudly took them home to our mom and dad.

Set 10: Focus on Verb Problems

@ Verb (Tense), Using the Right Word, Comma (Appositive)

Mr. Singh our ancient-history teacher learned us that the new names for Siam,

Mesopotamia, and Persia were Thailand, Iraq, and Iran.

@ Subject-Verb Agreement, Comma Splice, Capitalization, Using the Right Word

Not all people in the World considers black to be the color for mourning, in china

and in muslim countries, mourners ware white.

@ Subject-Verb Agreement, Verb (Tense), Sentence Fragment, Capitalization

Neither my Mother nor my Father have the answer to why tennis balls are fuzzy. Or

why golf balls had dimples.

@ Subject-Verb Agreement, End Punctuation, Comma (Other)

Blue and white is the most popular high school colors but are rock or country the

most popular music.

@ Pronoun-Antecedent Agreement, Using the Right Word, Plurals, Comma (Other)

When a person shivers, they increase the muscular activity in there bodys and that

helps them warm up.

Corrected Sentences

◎ Verb (Tense), Using the Right Word, Comma (Appositive)

Mr. Singh**,** our ancient-history teacher**,** ~~learned~~ *taught* us that the new names for Siam,

Mesopotamia, and Persia ~~were~~ *are* Thailand, Iraq, and Iran.

◎ Subject-Verb Agreement, Comma Splice, Capitalization, Using the Right Word

Not all people in the *W*orld ~~considers~~ *consider* black to be the color for mourning**.** *I*n *C*hina

and in *M*uslim countries, mourners ~~ware~~ *wear* white.

◎ Subject-Verb Agreement, Verb (Tense), Sentence Fragment, Capitalization

Neither my *m*other nor my *f*ather ~~have~~ *has* the answer to why tennis balls are fuzzy**.** *O*r

why golf balls ~~had~~ *have* dimples.

◎ Subject-Verb Agreement, End Punctuation, Comma (Other)

Blue and white ~~is~~ *are* the most popular high school colors**,** but ~~are~~ *is* rock or country the

most popular music**?**

◎ Pronoun-Antecedent Agreement, Using the Right Word, Plurals, Comma (Other)

When ~~a person shivers~~ *people shiver*, they increase the muscular activity in ~~there bodys~~ *their bodies***,*** and that

helps them warm up.

Rock 'n' Roll Is Here to Stay

@ Subject-Verb Agreement, Comma (Other), Spelling, Italics (Underlining), Comma Splice, Punctuation (Title), Numbers, Nonstandard Language

1   Disc jockey Alan Freed coined the term rock 'n' roll in 1951, but the music

2   really owe its soul to the black rithim and blues performers of the late 1940s.

3   Chuck Berry, Little Richard, Otis Redding and scores of others from many different

4   backgrounds and cultures is honored at the Rock and Roll Hall of Fame and

5   Museum. The museum opened in Cleveland in the fall of 1995. Both Little

6   Richard and Yoko Ono was on hand to help cut the opening ribbon, a high school

7   band playing Respect and a 16-foot Elvis puppet was part of the celebratory

8   parade. Neither parents nor reviewers from the 1950s could of dreamed that

9   someday public and private contributors would donate nearly 100,000,000 dollars to

10   make sure rock 'n' roll got their place in history.

@ Sentence Combining
Combine the sentence that begins in line 3 and the first sentence that begins in line 5 using a **relative pronoun**. (See page 706.2 in *Write Source* for an example.) Write your combined sentence below.

_____

_____

_____

_____

Corrected Paragraph

@ Subject-Verb Agreement, Comma (Other), Spelling, Italics (Underlining), Comma Splice, Punctuation (Title), Numbers, Nonstandard Language

1   Disc jockey Alan Freed coined the term rock 'n' roll in 1951, but the music

2   really ~~owe~~ *owes* its soul to the black ~~rithim~~ *rhythm* and blues performers of the late 1940s.

3   Chuck Berry, Little Richard, Otis Redding *,* and scores of others from many different

4   backgrounds and cultures ~~is~~ *are* honored at the Rock and Roll Hall of Fame and

5   Museum. The museum opened in Cleveland in the fall of 1995. Both Little

6   Richard and Yoko Ono ~~was~~ *were* on hand to help cut the opening ribbon, *and* a high school

7   band playing *"*Respect*"* and a 16-foot Elvis puppet ~~was~~ *were* part of the celebratory

8   parade. Neither parents nor reviewers from the 1950s could ~~of~~ *have* dreamed that

9   someday public and private contributors would donate nearly ~~100,000,000 dollars~~ *$100 million* to

10   make sure rock 'n' roll got ~~their~~ *its* place in history.

Note: *Compound words such as "rock and roll," "high school," and "rhythm and blues" may be hyphenated: rock-and-roll, high-school, rhythm-and-blues.*

@ **Sentence Combining**
Combine the sentence that begins in line 3 and the first sentence that begins in line 5 using a **relative pronoun**. (See page 706.2 in *Write Source* for an example.) Write your combined sentence below.

Chuck Berry, Little Richard, Otis Redding, and scores of others from many

different backgrounds and cultures are honored at the Rock and Roll Hall of

Fame and Museum, which opened in Cleveland in the fall of 1995.

Set 11: Focus on Verb Problems

@ Verb Tense, Comma Splice, Using the Right Word

In 1869, the Navajo population is less then 10,000, in the 2000 census, the population was nearly 300,000.

@ Subject-Verb Agreement, Comma (Other), Sentence Fragment, Numbers

2/3 of all adult Americans wears corrective lenses. Because of nearsightedness farsightedness or astigmatism.

@ Subject-Verb Agreement, Capitalization

One of the most daring performers of all time were a French performer named Blondin, who crossed niagara falls on a tightrope.

@ Verb Tense, Comma (Nonrestrictive Phrase or Clause), Capitalization

The mother language of queen Victoria who sits on the throne of England for 64 years is German.

@ Using the Right Word, Rambling Sentence, Shift in Construction, Subject-Verb Agreement

The longest mountain range on earth lays under the ocean and is called the Dolphin Rise and it extend from the Arctic to the Antarctic with peaks so high they sometimes rose above the ocean's surface.

Corrected Sentences

@ **Verb Tense, Comma Splice, Using the Right Word**

In 1869, the Navajo population ~~is~~ *was* less ~~then~~ *than* 10,000~~,~~*;* in the 2000 census, the population was nearly 300,000.

@ **Subject-Verb Agreement, Comma (Other), Sentence Fragment, Numbers**

Two-thirds ~~2/3~~ of all adult Americans ~~wears~~ *wear* corrective lenses~~,~~ *B*ecause of nearsightedness*,* farsightedness*,* or astigmatism.

@ **Subject-Verb Agreement, Capitalization**

One of the most daring performers of all time ~~were~~ *was* a French performer named Blondin, who crossed *N*iagara *F*alls on a tightrope.

@ **Verb Tense, Comma (Nonrestrictive Phrase or Clause), Capitalization**

The mother language of *Q*ueen Victoria*,* who ~~sit~~ *sat* on the throne of England for 64 years*,* ~~is~~ *was* German.

@ **Using the Right Word, Rambling Sentence, Shift in Construction, Subject-Verb Agreement**

The longest mountain range on earth ~~lays~~ *lies* under the ocean and is called the Dolphin Rise*.* ~~and~~ *It* ~~extend~~ *extends* from the Arctic to the Antarctic with peaks so high they sometimes ~~rose~~ *rise* above the ocean's surface.

Staying Balanced over the Falls

Verb (Irregular), Verb (Tense), Comma (Nonrestrictive Phrase or Clause), Capitalization, Subject-Verb Agreement, Comma (Other), Spelling, Using the Right Word, Pronoun Usage, Numbers, Hyphen

1   How many ways is their to cross niagara falls on a tightrope? These world

2   famous falls are 167 feet high. They are 2,600 feet wide. In the mid-nineteenth

3   centruy a performer named Blondin walked across niagara falls on a 3 inch

4   tightrope sitted down fried hisself an egg on a stove he brought with him laid

5   down on the rope and pretends to nap. On 1 ocasion Blondin asked for a

6   volonteer he could carry piggyback across the Falls. The only one to volonteer was

7   his manager who shook so violently that Blondin almost lost his balance. One of

8   his craziest stunts, though, were stationing a man below the Falls and having him

9   shoot holes threw a hat that Blondin held as he balance on the rope.

Sentence Combining

Combine the second sentence that begins in line 1 and the first sentence that begins in line 2 using **correlative conjunctions**. (See page 734.2 in *Write Source* for an example; also see page 734 for a list of correlative conjunctions.) Write your combined sentence below.

_____

_____

_____

_____

Corrected Paragraph

⊚ Verb (Irregular), Verb (Tense), Comma (Nonrestrictive Phrase or Clause), Capitalization, Subject-Verb Agreement, Comma (Other), Spelling, Using the Right Word, Pronoun Usage, Numbers, Hyphen

1   How many ways ~~is their~~ *are there* to cross ~~n~~iagara ~~f~~alls on a tightrope? These world-

2   famous falls are 167 feet high. They are 2,600 feet wide. In the mid-nineteenth

3   ~~centruy~~ *century,* a performer named Blondin walked across ~~n~~iagara ~~f~~alls on a 3-inch

4   tightrope, ~~sitted~~ *sat* down, fried ~~hisself~~ *himself* an egg on a stove he brought with him, ~~laid~~ *lay*

5   down on the rope, and ~~pretends~~ *pretended* to nap. On ~~1 ocasion~~ *one occasion,* Blondin asked for a

6   ~~volonteer~~ *volunteer* he could carry piggyback across the ~~f~~Falls. The only one to ~~volonteer~~ *volunteer* was

7   his manager, who shook so violently that Blondin almost lost his balance. One of

8   his craziest stunts, though, ~~were~~ *was* stationing a man below the ~~f~~Falls and having him

9   shoot holes ~~threw~~ *through* a hat that Blondin held as he ~~balance~~ *balanced* on the rope.

⊚ **Sentence Combining**

Combine the second sentence that begins in line 1 and the first sentence that begins in line 2 using **correlative conjunctions**. (See page 734.2 in *Write Source* for an example; also see page 734 for a list of correlative conjunctions.) Write your combined sentence below.

Not only are these world-famous falls 167 feet high, but they are also 2,600 feet

wide.

Writers INC pp. 95 and 548.2

Set 12: Focus on Adjective and Adverb Form

℮ Using the Right Word, Adjective Form

The black widow spider is more harmfuler to humans then any other spider is.

℮ Misplaced Modifier, Adjective Form

Sawdust produces ice that is more stronger and safer than normal ice sprinkled on top of a pond as it freezes.

℮ Using the Right Word, Spelling, Adjective Form

Microwave ovens may be popularer with colege students then with their parents.

℮ Misplaced Modifier, Using the Right Word, Capitalization

Tourists see many sites walking through times square in New York City.

℮ Using the Right Word, Comma (Other), Adverb Form

Anyways my friend, if your a male, your 70 times more likelier to be color-blind than a female is.

Corrected Sentences

◉ **Using the Right Word, Adjective Form**

The black widow spider is more ~~harmfuler~~ *harmful* to humans ~~then~~ *than* any other spider is.

◉ **Misplaced Modifier, Adjective Form**

Sawdust produces ice that is ~~more~~ stronger and safer than normal ice sprinkled on

top of a pond as it freezes.

◉ **Using the Right Word, Spelling, Adjective Form**

Microwave ovens may be ~~popularer~~ *more popular* with ~~colege~~ *college* students ~~then~~ *than* with their parents.

◉ **Misplaced Modifier, Using the Right Word, Capitalization**

t
Tourists see many ~~sites~~ *sights* *W*alking through *t*imes *s*quare in New York City,

◉ **Using the Right Word, Comma (Other), Adverb Form**

~~Anyways~~ *Anyway*, my friend, if ~~your~~ *you're* a male, ~~your~~ *you're* 70 times more ~~likelier~~ *likely* to be color-blind than

a female is.

The Microwave Bust

@ Adjective Form, Using the Right Word, Spelling, Comma (To Separate Adjectives), Subject-Verb Agreement, Comma (Other), Verb (Tense), Parallel Structure, Comma Splice

1   At one time, many people thought microwave ovens would become

2   most popular then any other household applyance. Microwave cooking would free

3   cooks from ours of labor, speed up cooking and not heat up a kitchen. Cooks would

4   be happy if they never again had to bend over to remove a hot heavy pan

5   from a conventional oven. Well the revolution never happened, many foods prepared

6   in a microwave just doesn't taste as good as foods baked in a conventional oven.

7   Also, the microwaved foods didn't have the same appearance as foods baked in a

8   conventional oven. Sure microwave popcorn is popular but many people has gone

9   back to cooking meals the old-fashioned way. Nowadays the microwave is use

10   mostly for reheating and to defrost.

@ Sentence Combining

Combine the sentences that begin in lines 5 and 7 using a **coordinating conjunction**. (See page 734 in *Write Source* for an example and a list of coordinating conjunctions.) Write your combined sentence below.

_____

_____

_____

_____

Corrected Paragraph

⊘ Adjective Form, Using the Right Word, Spelling, Comma (To Separate Adjectives), Subject-Verb Agreement, Comma (Other), Verb (Tense), Parallel Structure, Comma Splice

1   At one time, many people thought microwave ovens would become

2 ~~most~~ *more* popular ~~then~~ *than* any other household ~~applyance~~ *appliance*. Microwave cooking would free

3 cooks from ~~ours~~ *hours* of labor, speed up cooking⌃*,* and not heat up a kitchen. Cooks would

4 be happy if they never again had to bend over to remove a hot⌃*,* heavy pan

5 from a conventional oven. Well⌃*,* the revolution never happened*.* ⸂*M*⸃many foods prepared

6 in a microwave just ~~doesn't~~ *didn't* taste as good as foods baked in a conventional oven.

7 Also, the microwaved foods didn't have the same appearance as foods baked in a

8 conventional oven. Sure⌃*,* microwave popcorn is popular⌃*,* but many people ~~has~~ *have* gone

9 back to cooking meals the old-fashioned way. Nowadays⌃*,* the microwave is ~~use~~ *used*

10 mostly for reheating and ~~to defrost~~ *defrosting*.

⊘ **Sentence Combining**

Combine the sentences that begin in lines 5 and 7 using a **coordinating conjunction**. (See page 734 in *Write Source* for an example and a list of coordinating conjunctions.) Write your combined sentence below.

Many foods prepared in a microwave just didn't taste as good or have the same

appearance as foods baked in a conventional oven.

Set 13: Focus on Dangling Modifiers and Double Negatives

@ **Dangling Modifier, Using the Right Word**

When looking far into outer space, distant stars are viewed threw both time and space.

@ **Double Negative, Pronoun-Antecedent Agreement, Subject-Verb Agreement, Capitalization**

Sharks doesn't never get Cancer despite its famous appetite for everything including the kitchen sink.

@ **Dangling Modifier, Capitalization, Subject-Verb Agreement**

Studying American History, Custer and his men was defeated at little big horn by the sioux under the leadership of chief sitting bull.

@ **Double Negative, Capitalization, Using the Right Word**

Even if people no every martial art, they don't have no superpowers; they still need to use Common Sense to avoid dangerous situations.

@ **Using the Right Word, Abbreviation, Comma (Other), Comma Splice**

Would you lease a plot of land for 10 million years? Their is a lease for a plot of land next to Columb Barracks in Mullingar Ireland, which was signed on Dec. 3 1868 for 10 million years, a sewage tank has been placed on the plot of land.

Corrected Sentences

@ **Dangling Modifier, Using the Right Word**

When looking far into outer space, ∧*we view* distant stars ~~are viewed~~ *through* ~~threw~~ both time and

space.

@ **Double Negative, Pronoun-Antecedent Agreement, Subject-Verb Agreement, Capitalization**

Sharks *don't* ~~doesn't never~~ get *C*ancer despite *their* ~~its~~ famous appetite for everything including

the kitchen sink.

@ **Dangling Modifier, Capitalization, Subject-Verb Agreement**

Studying American *h*istory, ∧*I learned that* Custer and his men *were* ~~was~~ defeated at *L*ittle *B*ig *H*orn by the

*S*ioux under the leadership of *C*hief *S*itting *B*ull.

@ **Double Negative, Capitalization, Using the Right Word**

Even if people *know* ~~no~~ every martial art, they don't have ~~no~~ superpowers; they still need to

use *c*ommon *s*ense to avoid dangerous situations.

@ **Using the Right Word, Abbreviation, Comma (Other), Comma Splice**

Would you lease a plot of land for 10 million years? *There* ~~Their~~ is a lease for a plot of

land next to Columb Barracks in Mullingar, Ireland, which was signed on ~~Dec.~~ *December* 3, 1868,

for 10 million years; *A* sewage tank has been placed on the plot of land.

The Practically Perfect White Shark

@ Dangling Modifier, Double Negative, Comma (Other), Using the Right Word, Spelling, Subject-Verb Agreement

1   Most people don't want to get no close-up look at a shark. Looking closely at

2   sharks however teaches us much we can learn about health fitness and survival.

3   Sharks are practicly perfect killing and eating machines. They are a biological

4   success. Scientists study sharks too learn about immunity to disease. White sharks

5   don't get sick they don't have no natural enemies and they survives brain damage

6   better then any other creature in the world. Trying to descover the secrets behind

7   this amazing health record plenty of time and money are needed.

@ Sentence Combining

Combine the sentences that begin in line 3 using an **appositive**. (See page 610.1 in *Write Source* for an example.) Write your combined sentence below.

_____

_____

_____

_____

Corrected Paragraph

@ **Dangling Modifier, Double Negative, Comma (Other), Using the Right Word, Spelling, Subject-Verb Agreement**

1   Most people don't want to get ~~no~~ *a* close-up look at a shark. Looking closely at

2   sharks, however, teaches us much we can learn about health, fitness, and survival.

3   Sharks are ~~practicly~~ *practically* perfect killing and eating machines. They are a biological

4   success. Scientists study sharks ~~too~~ *to* learn about immunity to disease. White sharks

5   don't get sick, they don't have ~~no~~ *any* natural enemies, and they ~~survives~~ *survive* brain damage

6   better ~~then~~ *than* any other creature in the world. Trying to ~~descover~~ *discover* the secrets behind

7   this amazing health record, *scientists need* plenty of time and money ~~are needed~~.

@ **Sentence Combining**
Combine the sentences that begin in line 3 using an **appositive**. (See page 610.1 in *Write Source* for an example.) Write your combined sentence below.

Sharks, practically perfect killing and eating machines, are a biological success.

_____

_____

_____

Set 14: Focus on Using the Right Word

@ **Using the Right Word, Rambling Sentence, Pronoun-Antecedent Agreement**

The hummingbird is the only bird that may fly backward and they may stay in one spot by beating there wings very fast and may also fly sideways or take off straight upward.

@ **Using the Right Word, Punctuation (Title), Sentence Fragment**

Rachel Carson, who's book Silent Spring helped expose the harmful affects of pesticides in our "throwaway society." She is highly regarded between environmentalists.

@ **Using the Right Word, Comma (Other)**

Is it alright to except donations from everyone except family members or do we need to await farther instructions?

@ **Using the Right Word, Double Negative, Plurals, Adjective Form**

Perhaps the most fussy eater in the world is the beloved koala bear of Australia, whom won't eat nothing accept eucalyptus leafs.

@ **Using the Right Word, Punctuation (Title), Spelling**

Who did the writers at Musician magazine interview for they're book on rock musicians, and what lead them to those spacific performers?

Corrected Sentences

◉ Using the Right Word, Rambling Sentence, Pronoun-Antecedent Agreement

The hummingbird is the only bird that ~~may~~ *can* fly backward, and ~~they may~~ *It can* stay in one spot by beating ~~there~~ *its* wings very fast and ~~may~~ *can* also fly sideways or take off straight upward.

◉ Using the Right Word, Punctuation (Title), Sentence Fragment

Rachel Carson, ~~who's~~ *whose* book Silent Spring helped expose the harmful ~~affects~~ *effects* of pesticides in our "throwaway society," ~~She~~ is highly regarded ~~between~~ *among* environmentalists.

◉ Using the Right Word, Comma (Other)

Is it ~~alright~~ *all right* to ~~except~~ *accept* donations from everyone except family members, or do we need to await ~~farther~~ *further* instructions?

◉ Using the Right Word, Double Negative, Plurals, Adjective Form

Perhaps the ~~most fussy~~ *fussiest* eater in the world is the beloved koala bear of Australia, ~~whom~~ *who* won't eat ~~nothing accept~~ *anything except* eucalyptus ~~leafs~~ *leaves*.

◉ Using the Right Word, Punctuation (Title), Spelling

~~Who~~ *Whom* did the writers at Musician magazine interview for ~~they're~~ *their* book on rock musicians, and what ~~lead~~ *led* them to those ~~spacific~~ *specific* performers?

The Throwaway Society

Using the Right Word, End Punctuation, Plurals, Subject-Verb Agreement, Comma Splice, Spelling, Pronoun-Antecedent Agreement

1   Who's responsability is it to protect society and the envirment from the affects

2 of pollution and overconsumption? Is their any hope that we may change our

3 coarse. Who can we trust, who will led us in this area. The United States and

4 other highly developed countrys is in danger of being buried and poisoned by its

5 own waist. The majority of us pays little attention to how much garbage we

6 produce. We think its alright to buy products wrapped in layers of plastic and

7 polystyrene foam. Compatition in our neighborhoods for the *perfect* lawn leds us

8 to flood our property with harmful pesticides. It's time to stop the insanity. It's

9 time to except responsibility. It's time to prevent farther damage to the enviroment

10 before its to late.

Sentence Combining

Combine the sentences that begin in lines 8 and 9 using a **series**. (See page 610.2 in *Write Source* for an example.) Write your combined sentence below.

_____

_____

_____

_____

Corrected Paragraph

@ Using the Right Word, End Punctuation, Plurals, Subject-Verb Agreement, Comma Splice,
Spelling, Pronoun-Antecedent Agreement

1   *Whose responsibility*   *environment*   *effects*
     ~~Who's~~ ~~responsability~~ is it to protect society and the ~~envirment~~ from the ~~affects~~

2   of pollution and overconsumption? Is ~~their~~ *there* any hope that we ~~may~~ *can* change our

3   *course* ?*Whom*   *W*   *lead*   ?
     ~~coarse~~; ~~Who~~ can we trust who will ~~led~~ us in this area The United States and

4   *countries are*   *their*
     other highly developed ~~countrys~~ ~~is~~ in danger of being buried and poisoned by ~~its~~

5   *waste*   *pay*
     own ~~waist~~. The majority of us ~~pays~~ little attention to how much garbage we

6   *it's all right*
     produce. We think ~~its~~ ~~alright~~ to buy products wrapped in layers of plastic and

7   *Competition*   *leads*
     polystyrene foam. ~~Compatition~~ in our neighborhoods for the *perfect* lawn ~~leds~~ us

8   to flood our property with harmful pesticides. It's time to stop the insanity. It's

9   *accept*   *further*   *environment*
     time to ~~except~~ responsibility. It's time to prevent ~~farther~~ damage to the ~~enviroment~~

10   *it's too*
     before ~~its~~ ~~to~~ late.

@ Sentence Combining

Combine the sentences that begin in lines 8 and 9 using a **series**. (See page 610.2 in *Write
Source* for an example.) Write your combined sentence below.

It's time to stop the insanity, to accept responsibility, and to prevent further

damage to the environment before it's too late.

62

Set 15: Focus on Using the Right Word

◉ Using the Right Word, Comma (Nonrestrictive Phrase or Clause), Sentence Fragment

The blue whale who is the largest creature on Earth has a 1,200-pound heart. And blood vessels so large that a small child could crawl threw them.

◉ Using the Right Word, Double Negative, Run-On Sentence, Capitalization

Costa Rica, one of the few countries in the world that doesn't have no army, educates it's population good the central American country has a 96 percent literacy rate.

◉ Using the Right Word, Adverb Form, Capitalization, Nonstandard Language, Comma Splice

Would you borrow me your notes from that Social Studies lecture about the bill of rights, I should of listened more careful.

◉ Using the Right Word, Comma (Other), Hyphen

Are we already for a high tech future or is it already hear?

◉ Using the Right Word, Run-On Sentence, Spelling

To enjoy good health, you should try to maintain a positive mental additude tell yourself, when a bad thing happens, that this, two, shall pass.

Corrected Sentences

⊜ **Using the Right Word, Comma (Nonrestrictive Phrase or Clause), Sentence Fragment**

The blue whale, ~~who~~ *which* is the largest creature on Earth, has a 1,200-pound heart, ~~And~~ *a*

blood vessels so large that a small child could crawl ~~threw~~ *through* them.

⊜ **Using the Right Word, Double Negative, Run-On Sentence, Capitalization**

Costa Rica, one of the few countries in the world that ~~doesn't have~~ *has* no army, educates

~~it's~~ *its* population ~~good~~ *well*, the ~~c~~ *C*entral American country has a 96 percent literacy rate.

⊜ **Using the Right Word, Adverb Form, Capitalization, Nonstandard Language, Comma Splice**

Would you ~~borrow~~ *lend* me your notes from that ~~s~~ *S*ocial ~~s~~ *S*tudies lecture about the ~~b~~ *B*ill of

~~r~~ *R*ights? I should ~~of~~ *have* listened more ~~careful~~ *carefully*.

⊜ **Using the Right Word, Comma (Other), Hyphen**

Are we ~~already~~ *all ready* for a high-tech future, or is it already ~~hear~~ *here*?

⊜ **Using the Right Word, Run-On Sentence, Spelling**

To enjoy good health, you should try to maintain a positive mental ~~additude~~ *attitude*. *T*ell

yourself, when a bad thing happens, that this, ~~two,~~ *too*, shall pass.

The Price of Peace

@ Numbers, Run-On Sentence, Pronoun Usage, Shift in Construction, Comma (Other), Capitalization, Using the Right Word, Nonstandard Language, Spelling

1   Alfred Nobel was a swedish citizen. He succeeded as both an inventor and a

2 businessman he recieved 355 patents for his inventions and in the process built

3 hisself a fortune. However when his nitroglycerin factory blew up in 1864 killing 5

4 people including his brother Nobel is devastated. All ready a pacifist, perhaps he

5 should of halted his work with explosive chemicals. Instead he continued, and two

6 years later he invents dynamite. Nobel left his fortune to a foundation who

7 awards prizes for excellance in sevral fields. Its ironic too realize that the man

8 which invented dynamite is the man who funded the Nobel Peace Prize.

@ **Sentence Combining**
Combine the sentences that begin in line 1 using an **appositive**. (See page 610.1 in *Write Source* for an example.) Write your combined sentence below.

_____

_____

_____

_____

_____

Corrected Paragraph

@ Numbers, Run-On Sentence, Pronoun Usage, Shift in Construction, Comma (Other),
Capitalization, Using the Right Word, Nonstandard Language, Spelling

1   Alfred Nobel was a ~~s~~wedish citizen. He succeeded as both an inventor and a

2   businessman. ~~h~~e ~~recieved~~ *received* 355 patents for his inventions and in the process built

3   ~~hisself~~ *himself* a fortune. However, when his nitroglycerin factory blew up in 1864, killing ~~5~~ *five*

4   people, including his brother, Nobel ~~is~~ *was* devastated. ~~All ready~~ *Already* a pacifist, perhaps he

5   should ~~of~~ *have* halted his work with explosive chemicals. Instead he continued, and two

6   years later he ~~invents~~ *invented* dynamite. Nobel left his fortune to a foundation ~~who~~ *that*

7   awards prizes for ~~excellance~~ *excellence* in ~~sevral~~ *several* fields. ~~Its~~ *It's* ironic ~~too~~ *to* realize that the man

8   ~~which~~ *who* invented dynamite is the man who funded the Nobel Peace Prize.

@ **Sentence Combining**
Combine the sentences that begin in line 1 using an **appositive**. (See page 610.1 in *Write Source* for an example.) Write your combined sentence below.

Alfred Nobel, a Swedish citizen, succeeded as both an inventor and a

businessman.

Set 16: Mixed Review

@ Run-On Sentence, Abbreviation, Capitalization, Spelling, Comma (Other)

The avrage american generates 1000 lbs of recyclable garbage each year how much of this is actually recycled?

@ Abbreviation, Using the Right Word, Spelling, Shift in Construction

Paint acounts for about 60% of the hazardous waist that came from homes.

@ Hyphen, Using the Right Word, Plurals

By the year 2000, more then half of the kids in the United States had spent part of there lifes in single parent homes.

@ Parentheses, Using the Right Word, Run-On Sentence, Spelling

Oceans are as much as 90 percent barren compleatly without life they're like wet desserts.

@ Sentence Fragment, Capitalization, Adjective Form, Verb (Irregular)

We finded out in astronomy 101. That the planet earth is the heavier of all the planets in our solar system.

Corrected Sentences

𝒞 **Run-On Sentence, Abbreviation, Capitalization, Spelling, Comma (Other)**

The ~~avrage~~ *average* ^A^merican generates 1,000 ~~lbs~~ *pounds* of recyclable garbage each yea⬭ ^H^ow much of

this is actually recycled?

𝒞 **Abbreviation, Using the Right Word, Spelling, Shift in Construction**

Paint ~~acounts~~ *accounts* for about 60% *percent* of the hazardous ~~waist~~ *waste* that ~~came~~ *comes* from homes.

𝒞 **Hyphen, Using the Right Word, Plurals**

By the year 2000, more ~~then~~ *than* half of the kids in the United States had spent part of

~~there~~ *their* ~~lifes~~ *lives* in single‑parent homes.

𝒞 **Parentheses, Using the Right Word, Run-On Sentence, Spelling**

Oceans are as much as 90 percent barren (~~compleatly~~ *completely* without life) they're like wet

~~desserts~~ *deserts*.

𝒞 **Sentence Fragment, Capitalization, Adjective Form, Verb (Irregular)**

We ~~finded~~ *found* out in ^A^stronomy 101 ^t^hat the planet ^E^arth is the ~~heavier~~ *heaviest* of all the

planets in our solar system.

The Joy of Snorkeling

@ Subject-Verb Agreement, Using the Right Word, Abbreviation, Comma Splice, Spelling, Plurals, Sentence Fragment, Shift in Construction, Capitalization, Comma (Other), Dashes, Apostrophe

1   Snorkeling the coral reefs of the Flor. Keys are one way to explore coastal

2   waters. Snorkeling is swimming facedown near the waters surface. A mask

3   covering you're eyes and nose. Allows you to see. A snorkel tube—one end in your

4   mouth and the other end reaching above the water—allows you to breathe. For

5   a small fee you can rent a mask a snorkel tube and flippers. When entering the

6   water remember that you are in an enviroment unaccustomed to humans. Don't

7   touch the fish or the delicate corals and sea fans who abound in the sun-warmed

8   saltwater, some sea creatures portuguese man-of-wars, moon jellyfish and stingrays

9   delivers mild to life-threatening stings. Snorkeling gives me a close-up look at life

10 in the ocean. It learns you an appreshiation for the ocean's beauty and variety.

@ **Sentence Combining**

Combine the sentences that begin in lines 9 and 10 using an **introductory phrase**. (See page 610.3 in *Write Source* for an example.) Write your combined sentence below.

_____

_____

_____

_____

Corrected Paragraph

@ Subject-Verb Agreement, Using the Right Word, Abbreviation, Comma Splice, Spelling, Plurals, Sentence Fragment, Shift in Construction, Capitalization, Comma (Other), Dashes, Apostrophe

Florida *is*
1   Snorkeling the coral reefs of the ~~Flor.~~ Keys ~~are~~ one way to explore coastal

2   waters. Snorkeling is swimming facedown near the water's surface. A mask

your *a*
3   covering ~~you're~~ eyes and nose. ~~A~~llows you to see. A snorkel tube—one end in your

4   mouth and the other end reaching above the water—allows you to breathe. For

5   a small fee, you can rent a mask, a snorkel tube, and flippers. When entering the

environment
6   water, remember that you are in an ~~enviroment~~ unaccustomed to humans. Don't

that
7   touch the fish or the delicate corals and sea fans ~~who~~ abound in the sun-warmed

S *P* *men-of-war*
8   saltwater. ~~s~~ome sea creatures portuguese ~~man-of-wars~~, moon jellyfish, and stingrays—

deliver *you*
9   ~~delivers~~ mild to life-threatening stings. Snorkeling gives ~~me~~ a close-up look at life

teaches *appreciation*
10   in the ocean. It ~~learns~~ you an ~~appreshiation~~ for the ocean's beauty and variety.

@ **Sentence Combining**
Combine the sentences that begin in lines 9 and 10 using an **introductory phrase**. (See page 610.3 in *Write Source* for an example.) Write your combined sentence below.

By giving you a close-up look at life in the ocean, snorkeling teaches you an

appreciation for the ocean's beauty and variety.

Set 17: Mixed Review

✪ Capitalization, Comma Splice, Subject-Verb Agreement, Spelling

Laff, and the World laff with you, weep, and you weep alone.

✪ Adjective Form, Capitalization, Spelling, Parentheses, Apostrophe

Timbuktu Im sure youve heard of it is a really city in the african contrie of Mali.

✪ Verb (Irregular), Punctuation (Title), Capitalization

The Raven is the title of a Poem writed by the american author Edgar Allan Poe.

✪ Using the Right Word, Spelling, Numbers, Subject-Verb Agreement

Adult male tigers way about four hundred twenty pounds and is aproximatly 10 feet long.

✪ Punctuation (Title), Verb (Irregular), Sentence Fragment

Quasimodo is the central character in The Hunchback of Notre Dame. A novel wrote by Victor Hugo.

Corrected Sentences

@ **Capitalization, Comma Splice, Subject-Verb Agreement, Spelling**

Laugh   *w* *laughs*   y
~~Laff~~, and the World ~~laff~~ with you; weep, and you weep alone.

@ **Adjective Form, Capitalization, Spelling, Parentheses, Apostrophe**

                (v   v   )   *real*   *A*   *country*
Timbuktu Im sure youve heard of it is a ~~really~~ city in the african ~~contrie~~ of Mali.

@ **Verb (Irregular), Punctuation (Title), Capitalization**

"   "   *P* *written*   *A*
The Raven is the title of a Poem ~~writed~~ by the american author Edgar Allan Poe.

@ **Using the Right Word, Spelling, Numbers, Subject-Verb Agreement**

                     weigh   *420*   *are approximately*
Adult male tigers ~~way~~ about ~~four hundred twenty~~ pounds and ~~is aproximatly~~ 10 feet

long.

@ **Punctuation (Title), Verb (Irregular), Sentence Fragment**

                                                                    y *a*   *written*
Quasimodo is the central character in The Hunchback of Notre Dame, A novel ~~wrote~~

by Victor Hugo.

The Tragic Life of Edgar Allan Poe

@ Spelling, Hyphen, Shift in Construction, Capitalization, Apostrophe, Numbers, Comma (Other), Punctuation (Title), Comma Splice, Misplaced Modifier, Using the Right Word

1   Edgar Allan Poe suffered 2 tragadies before he was 3 years old. His mother

2   has dyed and his father has desserted the family. John Allan, his foster father did

3   not give Poe enuf money to pay for his education at the university of virginia and

4   Poe deeply in debt dropped out. He married his 13 year old cousin Virginia

5   Clemm who died young of tuberculosis. He was a brilliant editor and writer

6   because of his drinking and fighting but Poe was always poor and in trouble.

7   Many of his stories (like the Cask of Amontillado) have mystery, horror or death

8   themes, his poems (like Annabel Lee) often have themes of love and beauty. Poe

9   died at age forty broke and unappreciated, he is considered one of Americas'

10   greatest writers.

@ Sentence Combining
Combine the sentences that begin in line 1 using an **introductory clause**. (See page 610.3 in *Write Source* for an example.) Write your combined sentence below.

_____

_____

_____

_____

Corrected Paragraph

♐ Spelling, Hyphen, Shift in Construction, Capitalization, Apostrophe, Numbers, Comma (Other), **Punctuation (Title), Comma Splice, Misplaced Modifier, Using the Right Word**

1   Edgar Allan Poe suffered ~~2~~ *two* ~~tragadies~~ *tragedies* before he was ~~3~~ *three* years old. His mother

2   ~~has dyed~~ *had died*, and his father ~~has desserted~~ *had deserted* the family. John Allan, his foster father, did

3   not give Poe ~~enuf~~ *enough* money to pay for his education at the University of Virginia, and

4   Poe, deeply in debt, dropped out. He married his 13-year-old cousin, Virginia

5   Clemm, who died young of tuberculosis. He was a brilliant editor and writer,

6   (because of his drinking and fighting) but Poe was always poor and in trouble.

7   Many of his stories (like the "Cask of Amontillado") have mystery, horror, or death

8   themes, *while* his poems (like "Annabel Lee") often have themes of love and beauty. Poe

9   died at age ~~forty~~ *40* broke and unappreciated, *but* he is considered one of America's

10   greatest writers.

♐ **Sentence Combining**
Combine the sentences that begin in line 1 using an **introductory clause**. (See page 610.3 in *Write Source* for an example.) Write your combined sentence below.

Before Edgar Allan Poe was three years old, his mother had died, and his father

had deserted the family.

Set 18: Mixed Review

© **Comma (To Separate Adjectives), Spelling, Using the Right Word, Capitalization**

The blues is a kind of sad slow music that diveloped between african americans in the southern United States.

© **Sentence Fragment, Capitalization, Spelling, Hyphen, Comma (Other)**

Cathedrals are large, impressive christion churches. With high arches domed ceilings and stained glass windows.

© **Italics (Underlining), Verb (Irregular), Spelling**

The use of the term cool to mean somthing excellent growed in the 1960s.

© **Comma (Other), Numbers, Abbreviation**

At the turn of the twenty-first century more than fifty % of women ages 25 to 54 were working outside the home.

© **Shift in Construction, Using the Right Word, Capitalization, Sentence Fragment**

Johnny appleseed was the nickname of an american pioneer and folk hero. Who's real name is John Chapman.

Corrected Sentences

- **Comma (To Separate Adjectives), Spelling, Using the Right Word, Capitalization**

  The blues is a kind of sad, slow music that ~~diveloped between~~ *developed among* African Americans in the southern United States.

- **Sentence Fragment, Capitalization, Spelling, Hyphen, Comma (Other)**

  Cathedrals are large, impressive ~~christion~~ *Christian* churches with high arches, domed ceilings, and stained-glass windows.

- **Italics (Underlining), Verb (Irregular), Spelling**

  The use of the term _cool_ to mean ~~somthing~~ *something* excellent ~~growed~~ *grew* in the 1960s.

- **Comma (Other), Numbers, Abbreviation**

  At the turn of the twenty-first century, more than ~~fifty %~~ *50 percent* of women ages 25 to 54 were working outside the home.

- **Shift in Construction, Using the Right Word, Capitalization, Sentence Fragment**

  Johnny Appleseed was the nickname of an American pioneer and folk hero whose ~~Who's~~ real name ~~is~~ *was* John Chapman.

Isn't It Romanthic?

Ⓔ Comma (Nonrestrictive Phrase or Clause), Capitalization, Using the Right Word, Spelling, Hyphen, Run-On Sentence, Comma (To Separate Adjectives), Quotation Marks, Comma (Other)

1   Old English and European cathedrals built during the middle ages (1000–1500

2   C.E.) are often examples of Romanesque or Gothic arkitexture. With there thick

3   walls dark facades and small windows the earlier Romanesque cathedrals look

4   like fortresses. Gothic cathedrals which were built somewhat latter have

5   magnificent towering spires. They also are taller then the Romanesque churches.

6   Gothic cathedrals usualy have large colorful stained glass windows. Sometimes

7   building a cathedral ended up as a 200-year project. If a cathedral was destroyed

8   by fire, lightning or wars, it was often partially or completly rebuilt. Lincoln

9   cathedral in England for example is part Romanesque and part Gothic perhaps we

10   could call this style "Romanthic".

Ⓔ **Sentence Combining**
Combine the sentences that begin in lines 4 and 5 using a **coordinating conjunction**.
(See page 734 in *Write Source* for an example and a list of coordinating conjunctions.)
Write your combined sentence below.

_____

_____

_____

_____

Corrected Paragraph

@ Comma (Nonrestrictive Phrase or Clause), Capitalization, Using the Right Word, Spelling, Hyphen, Run-On Sentence, Comma (To Separate Adjectives), Quotation Marks, Comma (Other)

1   Old English and European cathedrals built during the *M**iddle* *A**ges* (1000–1500

2   C.E.) are often examples of Romanesque or Gothic ~~arkitexture~~ *architecture*. With ~~there~~ *their* thick

3   walls, dark facades, and small windows, the earlier Romanesque cathedrals look

4   like fortresses. Gothic cathedrals, which were built somewhat ~~latter~~ *later*, have

5   magnificent, towering spires. They also are taller ~~then~~ *than* the Romanesque churches.

6   Gothic cathedrals ~~usualy~~ *usually* have large, colorful stained-glass windows. Sometimes

7   building a cathedral ended up as a 200-year project. If a cathedral was destroyed

8   by fire, lightning, or wars, it was often partially or ~~completly~~ *completely* rebuilt. Lincoln

9   *C*athedral in England, for example, is part Romanesque and part Gothic, perhaps we

10   could call this style "Romanthic."

@ **Sentence Combining**
Combine the sentences that begin in lines 4 and 5 using a **coordinating conjunction**.
(See page 734 in *Write Source* for an example and a list of coordinating conjunctions.)
Write your combined sentence below.

Gothic cathedrals, which were built somewhat later, have magnificent, towering

spires and are taller than the Romanesque churches.

Writers INC p. 548

Set 19: Mixed Review

@ **Numbers, Comma (Appositive), Capitalization, Spelling**

Some scientists beleive that our home galaxy the milky way is about 12,000,000,000 years old.

@ **Abbreviation, Verb (Tense), Capitalization**

The Civil War came to an end in 1865 when Robert E Lee surrenders to Ulysses S Grant at appomattox Court House in Virginia.

@ **Sentence Fragment, Capitalization, Using the Right Word, Pronoun Usage, Article**

Tara and myself learned that a mirage is a optical allusion. Occurs in the dessert, in the arctic, and sometimes above hot pavement.

@ **Verb (Irregular), Quotation Marks, Capitalization**

Abraham Lincoln begun the gettysburg address by saying, fourscore and seven years ago, . . .

@ **Numbers, Adverb Form, Using the Right Word**

Fluorescent lightbulbs last thirteen times more long then regular incandescent bulbs.

Corrected Sentences

@ **Numbers, Comma (Appositive), Capitalization, Spelling**

Some scientists ~~beleive~~ *believe* that our home galaxy, the ~~m~~ilky ~~w~~ay, is about ~~12,000,000,000~~ *12 billion*
years old.

@ **Abbreviation, Verb (Tense), Capitalization**

The Civil War came to an end in 1865 when Robert E. Lee ~~surrenders~~ *surrendered* to Ulysses S. Grant at ~~a~~ppomattox Court House in Virginia.

@ **Sentence Fragment, Capitalization, Using the Right Word, Pronoun Usage, Article**

Tara and ~~myself~~ *I* learned that a mirage is ~~a~~ *an* optical ~~allusion~~ *illusion* ~~o~~ccurs *that* in the ~~dessert~~ *desert*, in the ~~a~~rctic, and sometimes above hot pavement.

@ **Verb (Irregular), Quotation Marks, Capitalization**

Abraham Lincoln ~~begun~~ *began* the ~~g~~ettysburg ~~a~~ddress by saying, "Fourscore and seven years ago, . . ."

@ **Numbers, Adverb Form, Using the Right Word**

Fluorescent lightbulbs last ~~thirteen~~ *13* times ~~more long~~ *longer* ~~then~~ *than* regular incandescent bulbs.

What Makes a Mirage?

℮ Using the Right Word, Comma Splice, Pronoun Usage, Comma (Other), Nonstandard Language, Pronoun-Antecedent Agreement, Comma (Parenthetical or Contrasted Elements), Spelling, End Punctuation, Subject-Verb Agreement, Hyphen

1   Do you remember those comic strips with the guy dragging hisself across the

2   dessert toward what he thinks is water, only too have it move on ahead of him.

3   The pour guy is seeing a mirage and the problem is optical not mental. A mirage

4   is actualy a reflection of light from the sky. It appears only when the temperature

5   is write. First their have to be a layer of hot air over a surface, at the same time

6   there must be a layer of cool air just above the hot air. Rays of light from the

7   sky go in a straight line thru the cool air but when they hit the hot air, it bends

8   upward and than into the eye. What looks like a pool of refreshing water is just

9   sky blue air, what a disappointment for a thirsty person!

℮ **Sentence Combining**
Combine the second sentence that begins in line 3 and the sentence that begins in line 4 using an **appositive**. (See page 610.1 in *Write Source* for an example.) Write your combined sentence below.

_____

_____

_____

_____

Corrected Paragraph

@ Using the Right Word, Comma Splice, Pronoun Usage, Comma (Other), Nonstandard Language, Pronoun-Antecedent Agreement, Comma (Parenthetical or Contrasted Elements), Spelling, End Punctuation, Subject-Verb Agreement, Hyphen

himself
1   Do you remember those comic strips with the guy dragging ~~hisself~~ across the

desert   *to*
2   ~~dessert~~ toward what he thinks is water, only ~~too~~ have it move ~~on~~ ahead of him**?**

poor
3   The ~~pour~~ guy is seeing a mirage, and the problem is optical, not mental. A mirage

actually
4   is ~~actualy~~ a reflection of light from the sky. It appears only when the temperature

right   *there has*
5   is ~~write~~. First ~~their~~ ~~have~~ to be a layer of hot air over a surface; at the same time,

6   there must be a layer of cool air just above the hot air. Rays of light from the

through   *they bend*
7   sky go in a straight line ~~thru~~ the cool air, but when they hit the hot air, ~~it bends~~

then
8   upward and ~~than~~ into the eye. What looks like a pool of refreshing water is just

W
9   sky-blue air. ~~what~~ a disappointment for a thirsty person!

@ **Sentence Combining**
Combine the second sentence that begins in line 3 and the sentence that begins in line 4 using an **appositive**. (See page 610.1 in *Write Source* for an example.) Write your combined sentence below.

A mirage, a reflection of light from the sky, appears only when the temperature is

right.

Set 20: Mixed Review

@ **Comma Splice, Capitalization, Using the Right Word, Hyphen**

Taiwan is a mountainous island that lays 90 miles off the coast of china in the south china sea, it is one of the high tech capitols of the world.

@ **Capitalization, Comma (Other), Using the Right Word, Comma (Unnecessary), Comma Splice**

The Talmud is a collection of jewish laws, and scholarly interpretations of they're meanings, it includes the books of genesis, exodus, leviticus, numbers and deuteronomy.

@ **Sentence Fragment, Comma (Other), Spelling, Pronoun-Antecedent Agreement**

Some tarantulas live more than 20 years grow large enough to eat small birds. And inject enuf poison into a victim to kill them.

@ **Using the Right Word, Comma (Other), Verb (Tense), Numbers**

Wild tea plants may grow as high as 30 feet but commercial tea plants were pruned to stay about three feet tall.

@ **Numbers, Comma (Other), Verb (Irregular)**

3,000,000 Americans fighted in the Civil War and 600,000 died in it.

Corrected Sentences

Comma Splice, Capitalization, Using the Right Word, Hyphen

Taiwan is a mountainous island that ~~lays~~ *lies* 90 miles off the coast of *C*hina in the *S*outh *C*hina *S*ea. *I*t is one of the high-tech ~~capitols~~ *capitals* of the world.

Capitalization, Comma (Other), Using the Right Word, Comma (Unnecessary), Comma Splice

The Talmud is a collection of *J*ewish laws and scholarly interpretations of ~~they're~~ *their* meanings; it includes the books of *G*enesis, *E*xodus, *L*eviticus, *N*umbers, and *D*euteronomy.

Sentence Fragment, Comma (Other), Spelling, Pronoun-Antecedent Agreement

Some tarantulas live more than 20 years, grow large enough to eat small birds, *a*nd inject ~~enuf~~ *enough* poison into a victim to kill ~~them~~ *it*.

Using the Right Word, Comma (Other), Verb (Tense), Numbers

Wild tea plants ~~may~~ *can* grow as high as 30 feet, but commercial tea plants ~~were~~ *are* pruned to stay about ~~three~~ *3* feet tall.

Numbers, Comma (Other), Verb (Irregular)

~~3,000,000~~ *Three million* Americans ~~fighted~~ *fought* in the Civil War, and 600,000 died in it.

Low-Tech Farming in a High-Tech Society

🌀 Using the Right Word, Comma (Other), Numbers, Capitalization, Dash, Subject-Verb Agreement, Hyphen

1   1/5 of the 20,000,000 people which live in taiwan are farmers. Although

2 machines have become popular, many taiwanese farmers still use the Water Buffalo.

3 The water buffalo easily climbs hillsides to plow fields. The stepped hillsides

4 provides more area to grow crops and by using fertilizers, a farmer is able to get

5 2 or 3 crops from one field during one growing season. Rice fruits peanuts and

6 tea is some main crops. Pigs, chickens, and ducks are common livestock.

7 Computers transistors and other technological products these manufactured items

8 are what we may associate with taiwan but its also a land of labor intensive

9 farming.

🌀 **Sentence Combining**
Combine the second sentence that begins in line 1 and the first sentence that begins in line 3 using a **relative pronoun**. (See page 704 in *Write Source* for an example.) Write your combined sentence below.

_____

_____

_____

_____

Corrected Paragraph

@ Using the Right Word, Comma (Other), Numbers, Capitalization, Dash, Subject-Verb Agreement, Hyphen

1   *One-fifth* ~~1/5~~ of the *20 million* ~~20,000,000~~ people ~~which~~ *who* live in ~~t~~*T*aiwan are farmers. Although

2   machines have become popular, many ~~t~~*T*aiwanese farmers still use the ~~W~~*w*ater ~~B~~*b*uffalo.

3   The water buffalo easily climbs hillsides to plow fields. The stepped hillsides

4   ~~provides~~ *provide* more area to grow crops, and by using fertilizers, a farmer is able to get

5   ~~2~~ *two* or ~~3~~ *three* crops from one field during one growing season. Rice, fruits, peanuts, and

6   tea ~~is~~ *are* some main crops. Pigs, chickens, and ducks are common livestock.

7   Computers, transistors, and other technological products—these manufactured items

8   are what we may associate with ~~t~~*T*aiwan, but ~~its~~ *it's* also a land of labor-intensive

9   farming.

@ **Sentence Combining**
Combine the second sentence that begins in line 1 and the first sentence that begins in line 3 using a **relative pronoun**. (See page 704 in *Write Source* for an example.) Write your combined sentence below.

Although machines have become popular, many Taiwanese farmers still use the

water buffalo, which easily climbs hillsides to plow fields.

Writers INC p. 95

Set 21: Mixed Review

⊘ **Subject-Verb Agreement, Capitalization, Using the Right Word, Spelling**

Abraham Lincoln were the first prominint leader in American History to favor giving

women the rite too vote.

⊘ **Run-On Sentence, Using the Right Word, Subject-Verb Agreement**

John F. Kennedy was notorious for asking people to borrow him money he were

always forgetting to bring cash with him to pay for restaurant checks and cab fares.

⊘ **Using the Right Word, Abbreviation, Apostrophe**

Its a rule that know living persons picture can appear on U.S. currency.

⊘ **Comma (Other), Capitalization, Using the Right Word**

Their are still a few regions on earth that have never been fully explored by people

among them the amazonian and african jungles.

⊘ **Comma (Other), Subject-Verb Agreement, Spelling, Using the Right Word**

Beleive it or not there is land crabs in Cuba that have the ability to run faster then

horses.

Corrected Sentences

Subject-Verb Agreement, Capitalization, Using the Right Word, Spelling

Abraham Lincoln ~~were~~ *was* the first ~~prominint~~ *prominent* leader in American *H*istory to favor giving women the ~~rite~~ *right* ~~too~~ *to* vote.

Run-On Sentence, Using the Right Word, Subject-Verb Agreement

John F. Kennedy was notorious for asking people to ~~borrow~~ *lend* him money*;* he ~~were~~ *was* always forgetting to bring cash with him to pay for restaurant checks and cab fares.

Using the Right Word, Abbreviation, Apostrophe

~~Its~~ *It's* a rule that ~~know~~ *no* living person*'*s picture ~~can~~ *may* appear on ~~U.S.~~ *United States* currency.

Comma (Other), Capitalization, Using the Right Word

~~Their~~ *There* are still a few regions on earth that have never been fully explored by people*,* among them the *A*mazonian and *A*frican jungles.

Comma (Other), Subject-Verb Agreement, Spelling, Using the Right Word

~~Beleive~~ *Believe* it or not*,* there ~~is~~ *are* land crabs in Cuba that have the ability to run faster ~~then~~ *than* horses.

Insects Rule

◉ Subject-Verb Agreement, Comma Splice, Article, Pronoun Usage, Using the Right Word, Plurals, Numbers, Comma (Other), Capitalization, Sentence Fragment, Comma (To Separate Adjectives)

1   Monkies and parrots may dominate the treetops of the jungle but it is the

2   smaller often invisible creatures who vastly outnumbers the mammals and birds.

3   Millions of leafcutter ants can make anthills sixteen feet deep and a acre wide,

4   termites bore down into the ground as far as one hundred and thirty feet looking

5   for the water table. While thousands of beetles forage through dead leafs in the

6   undergrowth. Insects like the walking stick and leafbug effectively camouflage itself

7   in the foliage. Colorful butterflies look like pieces of a rainbow. They flutter threw

8   a canopy of vines. Insects may be tiny in size but by there sheer numbers they

9   rule the jungle.

◉ **Sentence Combining**
Combine the sentences that begin in line 7 using a **participial phrase**. (See page 726.3 in *Write Source* for an example.) Write your combined sentence below.

_____

_____

_____

_____

Corrected Paragraph

⟲ Subject-Verb Agreement, Comma Splice, Article, Pronoun Usage, Using the Right Word, Plurals, Numbers, Comma (Other), Capitalization, Sentence Fragment, Comma (To Separate Adjectives)

Monkeys
1   ~~Monkies~~ and parrots may dominate the treetops of the jungle, but it is the

that   *outnumber*
2   smaller, often invisible creatures ~~who~~ vastly ~~outnumbers~~ the mammals and birds.

16   *an*
3   Millions of leafcutter ants can make anthills ~~sixteen~~ feet deep and ~~a~~ acre wide. .

T   *130*
4   termites bore down into the ground as far as ~~one hundred and thirty~~ feet looking

w   *leaves*
5   for the water table. While thousands of beetles forage through dead ~~leafs~~ in the

themselves
6   undergrowth. Insects like the walking stick and leafbug effectively camouflage ~~itself~~

through
7   in the foliage. Colorful butterflies look like pieces of a rainbow. They flutter ~~threw~~

their
8   a canopy of vines. Insects may be tiny in size, but by ~~there~~ sheer numbers they

9   rule the jungle.

⟲ **Sentence Combining**
Combine the sentences that begin in line 7 using a **participial phrase**. (See page 726.3 in *Write Source* for an example.) Write your combined sentence below.

Looking like pieces of a rainbow, colorful butterflies flutter through a canopy of

vines.

Writers INC p. 95

Set 22: Mixed Review

@ Comma (Other), Colon, Subject-Verb Agreement, Capitalization

Chariot races gladiator fights mock sea battles all these was popular events in the famous Colosseum of Ancient Rome.

@ Subject-Verb Agreement, Comma (Nonrestrictive Phrase or Clause), Nonstandard Language

Our solar system complete with the sun and planets are traveling acrost the Milky Way at about 180 miles per second.

@ Capitalization, Dangling Modifier

At the age of 26, while working in a swiss patent office as a clerk, the Theory of Relativity was developed by Albert Einstein.

@ Apostrophe, Subject-Verb Agreement, Deadwood/Wordiness, Capitalization

The fresh water frozen in earths frozen glaciers are hypothesized or estimated to be equal to about 60 years rainfall over the whole, entire planet.

@ Comma (Appositive), Italics (Underlining), Capitalization, Comma (Unnecessary)

In the hispanic culture, some people consider tuesday an unlucky day, perhaps because, the spanish word for tuesday—martes—comes from Mars the roman god of war.

Note: Days of the week are not capitalized in Spanish.

Corrected Sentences

◉ **Comma (Other), Colon, Subject-Verb Agreement, Capitalization**

Chariot races‸gladiator fights‸mock sea battles‸all these ~~was~~ *were* popular events in the famous Colosseum of *a*Ancient Rome.

◉ **Subject-Verb Agreement, Comma (Nonrestrictive Phrase or Clause), Nonstandard Language**

Our solar system‸complete with the sun and planets‸ ~~are~~ *is* traveling ~~acrost~~ *across* the Milky Way at about 180 miles per second.

◉ **Capitalization, Dangling Modifier**

At the age of 26, while working in a *S*swiss patent office as a clerk,‸*Albert Einstein developed* the *t*Theory of *r*Relativity ~~was developed by Albert Einstein.~~

◉ **Apostrophe, Subject-Verb Agreement, Deadwood/Wordiness, Capitalization**

The fresh water frozen in *E*earth's ~~frozen~~ glaciers ~~are hypothesized or~~ *is* estimated to be equal to about 60 years' rainfall over the ~~whole,~~ entire planet.

◉ **Comma (Appositive), Italics (Underlining), Capitalization, Comma (Unnecessary)**

In the *H*hispanic culture, some people consider *T*tuesday an unlucky day, perhaps because the *S*spanish word for *T*tuesday—*martes*—comes from Mars‸the *R*roman god of war.

That's Entertainment

@ Comma (Parenthetical or Contrasted Elements), Misplaced Modifier, Shift in Construction, Capitalization, Sentence Fragment, Subject-Verb Agreement, Abbreviation, Apostrophe, Using the Right Word

1   The romans built many outdoor arenas for recreational events, including the

2   famous colosseum in Rome. On its benches, the tall, four-story oval structure could

3   seat 50,000 spectators. For more than 300 years until the year 400 CE people

4   cheer as gladiators fight bloody man-to-man or man-against-animal battles to the

5   death. The Colosseum could also be partially filled with water. For mock sea

6   batles. Each ships crew attempted to sink there competitors. The crowd would go

7   wild. The Colosseum's Chariot races was also very popular. Today, inhabited only

8   by stray cats, the colosseum stands as a silent reminder of the noisy, violent

9   contests that thrilled Ancient Rome.

@ **Sentence Combining**
Combine the sentences that begin in line 6 using a **subordinating conjunction**. (See page 734 in *Write Source* for a list of subordinating conjunctions.) Write your combined sentence below.

_____

_____

_____

_____

Corrected Paragraph

@ Comma (Parenthetical or Contrasted Elements), Misplaced Modifier, Shift in Construction, Capitalization, Sentence Fragment, Subject-Verb Agreement, Abbreviation, Apostrophe, Using the Right Word

1   The *R*omans built many outdoor arenas for recreational events, including the

2 famous *C*olosseum in Rome. *O*n its benches, *T*he tall, four-story oval structure could

3 seat 50,000 spectators. For more than 300 years, until the year 400 C.E., people

4 *cheered* cheer as gladiators *fought* fight bloody man-to-man or man-against-animal battles to the

5 death. The Colosseum could also be partially filled with water, *f*or mock sea

6 *battles* batles. Each ship's crew attempted to sink *their* there competitors. The crowd would go

7 wild. The Colosseum's *c*hariot races *were* was also very popular. Today, inhabited only

8 by stray cats, the *C*olosseum stands as a silent reminder of the noisy, violent

9 contests that thrilled *a*ncient Rome.

@ **Sentence Combining**

Combine the sentences that begin in line 6 using a **subordinating conjunction**. (See page 734 in *Write Source* for a list of subordinating conjunctions.) Write your combined sentence below.

As each ship's crew attempted to sink their competitors, the crowd would go wild.

Set 23: Mixed Review

@ **Comma (Appositive), Subject-Verb Agreement, Article**

Chan Thomas a eminent geologist estimates that there has been 300 world floods and that there will be 300 more.

@ **Capitalization, Apostrophe, Abbreviation**

South american Water Hogs can weigh up to 50 lbs; they are the worlds largest rodents.

@ **Double Negative, Using the Right Word, Sentence Fragment**

Hetty Green was not only a shrewd and successful businessperson but also an eccentric tightwad whom once withheld medical treatment from her son. Because she didn't want to pay no hospital bill.

@ **Comma (To Separate Adjectives), Pronoun-Antecedent Agreement**

Gila monsters are large poisonous lizards whose tails hold substantial reserve food supplies that it can live off for months.

@ **Run-On Sentence, Using the Right Word, Comma (Other), Spelling**

Hitler had two Mercedes Benz cars specially equiped for his personnel use they were fitted with bulletproof glass and 2000 pounds of armor plate.

Corrected Sentences

@ **Comma (Appositive), Subject-Verb Agreement, Article**

Chan Thomas, *an* ~~a~~ eminent geologist, estimates that there *have* ~~has~~ been 300 world floods and

that there will be 300 more.

@ **Capitalization, Apostrophe, Abbreviation**

South *A*merican *W*ater *H*ogs can weigh up to 50 *pounds* ~~lbs~~; they are the world's largest

rodents.

@ **Double Negative, Using the Right Word, Sentence Fragment**

Hetty Green was not only a shrewd and successful businessperson but also an

eccentric tightwad *who* ~~whom~~ once withheld medical treatment from her son *b*ecause she

didn't want to pay *the* ~~no~~ hospital bill.

@ **Comma (To Separate Adjectives), Pronoun-Antecedent Agreement**

Gila monsters are large, poisonous lizards whose tails hold substantial reserve food

supplies that *they* ~~it~~ can live off for months.

@ **Run-On Sentence, Using the Right Word, Comma (Other), Spelling**

Hitler had two Mercedes Benz cars specially *equipped* ~~equiped~~ for his *personal* ~~personnel~~ use; they were

fitted with bulletproof glass and 2,000 pounds of armor plate.

Rich and Poor

✐ Verb (Tense), Using the Right Word, Comma (Other), Numbers, Nonstandard Language, Apostrophe, Rambling Sentence, Plurals, Run-On Sentence, Capitalization

1 In 1835, Hetty Green inherited her families fortune from the shipping and

2 whaling industrys. Hetty was a shrewd businessperson but she was also a

3 tightwad she wore raggedy clothes and lives in a tumbledown home in Hoboken

4 New Jersey. Her son's knee became infected. She took him to Bellevue hospital as

5 a charity patient. When the hospital found out whom she was they demanded

6 payment and rather than pay as she should of, Hetty withheld farther medical

7 treatment from her son and several years later he had to have his leg amputated.

8 At her death Hetty Greens estate was valued at $100,000,000.

✐ **Sentence Combining**
Combine the sentences that begin in line 4 using an **introductory clause**. (See page 610.3 in *Write Source* for an example.) Write your combined sentence below.

_____

_____

_____

_____

Writers INC p. 95

© Great Source. All rights reserved. (10)

Corrected Paragraph

@ Verb (Tense), **Using the Right Word**, Comma (Other), Numbers, Nonstandard Language, Apostrophe, Rambling Sentence, Plurals, Run-On Sentence, Capitalization

1   In 1835, Hetty Green inherited her ~~families~~ *family's* fortune from the shipping and

2 whaling ~~industrys~~ *industries*. Hetty was a shrewd businessperson, but she was also a

3 tightwad, she wore raggedy clothes and ~~lives~~ *lived* in a tumbledown home in Hoboken,

4 New Jersey. Her son's knee became infected. She took him to Bellevue *H*ospital as

5 a charity patient. When the hospital found out ~~whom~~ *who* she was, they demanded

6 payment, ~~and~~ *R*ather than pay as she should ~~of~~ *have*, Hetty withheld ~~farther~~ *further* medical

7 treatment from her son, and several years later he had to have his leg amputated.

8 At her death, Hetty Green*'s* estate was valued at $~~100,000,000~~ *100 million*.

@ **Sentence Combining**
Combine the sentences that begin in line 4 using an **introductory clause**. (See page 610.3 in *Write Source* for an example.) Write your combined sentence below.

When her son's knee became infected, she took him to Bellevue Hospital as a

charity patient.

Set 24: Mixed Review

@ **Subject-Verb Agreement, Using the Right Word, Abbreviation, Apostrophe**

Fewer than 20 percent of an avg. adult males weight come from his bones.

@ **Using the Right Word, Run-On Sentence, Comma (Other), Fair Language, Article**

A baby is likely to have 300 bones at berth but she will have only 206 bones as a adult as humans grow, their bones fuse.

@ **Punctuation (Title), Using the Right Word, Comma (Other)**

The famous "running of the bulls" in Pamplona Spain was popularized buy Ernest Hemingway in his novel Fiesta.

@ **Run-On Sentence, Comma (Other), Using the Right Word, Hyphen**

In 1894, the first major auto race was held on a coarse between Paris and Rouen France a steam driven car with a top speed of 11 miles per hour won the race.

@ **Numbers, Spelling, Comma (Unnecessary)**

In February, 1927, Babe Ruth hit one hundred twenty-five home runs in one hour, before an exhibation game in Los Angeles.

Corrected Sentences

@ **Subject-Verb Agreement, Using the Right Word, Abbreviation, Apostrophe**

Less   *average*   '/   *comes*
~~Fewer~~ than 20 percent of an ~~avg.~~ adult males weight ~~come~~ from his bones.

@ **Using the Right Word, Run-On Sentence, Comma (Other), Fair Language, Article**

                              birth   *or he*   *an*
A baby is likely to have 300 bones at ~~berth~~ but she will have only 206 bones as ~~a~~

adult as humans grow, their bones fuse.

@ **Punctuation (Title), Using the Right Word, Comma (Other)**

                                                               by
The famous "running of the bulls" in Pamplona, Spain, was popularized ~~buy~~ Ernest

Hemingway in his novel <u>Fiesta</u>.

@ **Run-On Sentence, Comma (Other), Using the Right Word, Hyphen**

                                        course
In 1894, the first major auto race was held on a ~~coarse~~ between Paris and Rouen,

   A
France. a steam-driven car with a top speed of 11 miles per hour won the race.

@ **Numbers, Spelling, Comma (Unnecessary)**

                                   125
In February, 1927, Babe Ruth hit ~~one hundred twenty-five~~ home runs in one hour,

            exhibition
before an ~~exhabition~~ game in Los Angeles.

Hardworking Bones

℮ Abbreviation, Run-On Sentence, Adverb Form, Comma (Parenthetical or Contrasted Elements), End Punctuation, Comma (Unnecessary), Subject-Verb Agreement, Nonstandard Language, Adjective Form, Comma (Other)

1   The human skeleton is strong. It supports one's entire body. Despite that, it

2   accounts for less than 20% of our body weight. Males as a general rule have 30%

3   more bone than females do. Bones have four main functions. First and second,

4   bones support the body and protects various organs for example the skull protects

5   the brain and the rib cage protects the heart and other organs. Third bones make

6   movement possible at the joints where two bones meet. Finally, bones produce red

7   blood cells, and store inorganic salts like calcium and phosphate. Bones get more

8   stronger with exercise and with use. If you're lazy your bones will thin out and

9   break more easy so get off of your tailbone and start moving

℮ **Sentence Combining**
Combine the first two sentences that begin in line 1 using a **semicolon**. (See page 618.1 in *Write Source* for an example.) Write your combined sentence below.

_____

_____

_____

Corrected Paragraph

℮ Abbreviation, Run-On Sentence, Adverb Form, Comma (Parenthetical or Contrasted Elements), End Punctuation, Comma (Unnecessary), Subject-Verb Agreement, Nonstandard Language, Adjective Form, Comma (Other)

1   The human skeleton is strong. It supports one's entire body. Despite that, it

2   accounts for less than 20% *percent* of our body weight. Males, as a general rule, have 30% *percent*

3   more bone than females do. Bones have four main functions. First and second,

4   bones support the body and ~~protects~~ *protect* various organs; for example, the skull protects

5   the brain, and the rib cage protects the heart and other organs. Third, bones make

6   movement possible at the joints where two bones meet. Finally, bones produce red

7   blood cells, and store inorganic salts like calcium and phosphate. Bones get ~~more~~

8   stronger with exercise and with use. If you're lazy, your bones will thin out and

9   break more ~~easy~~ *easily*, so get off ~~of~~ your tailbone and start moving!

℮ **Sentence Combining**
Combine the first two sentences that begin in line 1 using a **semicolon**. (See page 618.1 in *Write Source* for an example.) Write your combined sentence below.

The human skeleton is strong, strong enough to support one's entire body.

Set 25: Mixed Review

@ **Capitalization, Comma (Appositive), Article, Plurals**

Brigham Young a early leader of the mormons had 27 wifes, 16 of whom bore him children.

@ **Comma Splice, Using the Right Word, Pronoun-Antecedent Agreement, Spelling**

Barracudas are terrific swimers, it can attain swiming speeds faster then 60 miles per hour.

@ **Comma (Other), Capitalization, Subject-Verb Agreement, Hyphen**

Leonardo da Vinci Jack the ripper and president Harry Truman was all left handed.

@ **Capitalization, Comma (Other), Comma Splice, Plurals**

Jerusalem is one of the oldest citys in the world but the City of Gaziantep turkey is the oldest city in the World, it was founded around 3650 b.c.e.

@ **Italics (Underlining), Spelling, Comma (Parenthetical or Contrasted Elements)**

The term ophidiophobia refers to an exsesive or some people would say irrational fear of snakes.

Corrected Sentences

Capitalization, Comma (Appositive), Article, Plurals

Brigham Young, *an* ~~a~~ early leader of the *M*mormons, had 27 ~~wifes~~ *wives*, 16 of whom bore him children.

Comma Splice, Using the Right Word, Pronoun-Antecedent Agreement, Spelling

Barracudas are terrific ~~swimers~~ *swimmers*; ~~it~~ *they* can attain ~~swiming~~ *swimming* speeds faster ~~then~~ *than* 60 miles per hour.

Comma (Other), Capitalization, Subject-Verb Agreement, Hyphen

Leonardo da Vinci, Jack the *R*ripper, and *P*president Harry Truman ~~was~~ *were* all left-handed.

Capitalization, Comma (Other), Comma Splice, Plurals

Jerusalem is one of the oldest ~~citys~~ *cities* in the world, but the *C*City of Gaziantep, *T*turkey, is the oldest city in the *W*World; it was founded around 3650 *BCE* ~~b.c.e.~~

Italics (Underlining), Spelling, Comma (Parenthetical or Contrasted Elements)

The term ophidiophobia refers to an ~~exsesive~~ *excessive*, or some people would say irrational, fear of snakes.

A Sacred Rock in Jerusalem

@ Comma (Nonrestrictive Phrase or Clause), Colon, Apostrophe, Using the Right Word, Numbers, Comma (Appositive), Plurals, Comma (Other), Abbreviations

1 Jerusalem one of the oldest citys in the world is the home of a large granite

2 rock that is sacred to 3 major religions Judaism Christianity and Islam. The

3 famous rock measures 60 by forty feet. Jews claim that the rock is the place

4 where Abraham was sent to sacrifice his son Isaac (the sacrifice by the way never

5 happened because an angel intervened) and that it is the original sight of King

6 Solomons temple which was built around 900 B.C.E. According to Christianity

7 Jesus once preached a sermon on the rock. Islamic believers erected a domed

8 mosque over the rock in 691 ce. They say that the prophet Mohammed landed on

9 the rock after his famous Night Flight on the back of a winged hoarse.

@ Sentence Combining
Combine the sentences that begin in lines 7 and 8 using a **relative pronoun**. (See page 704 in *Write Source* for an example.) Write your combined sentence below.

_____

_____

_____

_____

Corrected Paragraph

@ Comma (Nonrestrictive Phrase or Clause), Colon, Apostrophe, Using the Right Word, Numbers, Comma (Appositive), Plurals, Comma (Other), Abbreviations

1   Jerusalem, one of the oldest ~~citys~~ *cities* in the world, is the home of a large granite

2 rock that is sacred to ~~3~~ *three* major religions, Judaism, Christianity, and Islam. The

3 famous rock measures 60 by ~~forty~~ *40* feet. Jews claim that the rock is the place

4 where Abraham was sent to sacrifice his son Isaac (the sacrifice, by the way, never

5 happened because an angel intervened) and that it is the original ~~sight~~ *site* of King

6 Solomon's temple, which was built around 900 B.C.E. According to Christianity,

7 Jesus once preached a sermon on the rock. Islamic believers erected a domed

8 mosque over the rock in 691 *C.E.* They say that the prophet Mohammed landed on

9 the rock after his famous Night Flight on the back of a winged ~~hoarse~~ *horse*.

@ **Sentence Combining**

Combine the sentences that begin in lines 7 and 8 using a **relative pronoun**. (See page 704 in *Write Source* for an example.) Write your combined sentence below.

Islamic believers, who erected a domed mosque over the rock in 691 C.E., say that

the prophet Mohammed landed on the rock after his famous Night Flight on the

back of a winged horse.

Writers INC p. 95

Set 26: Mixed Review

℮ **Comma (Other), Numbers, Spelling, Colon, Hyphen, Article**

"Diamond Jim" Brady, a American businessman, once ate the following for dinner 6 lobsters 2 ducks 30 oysters a sirloin steak vegtables 2 quarts of orange juice several pastries and a 2 pound box of candy.

℮ **Verb (Tense), Capitalization, Comma (Other), Using the Right Word**

Nellie Bly was a famous Investigative Reporter whom exposes american slums sweatshops jails and insane asylums in the late 1800s.

℮ **Sentence Fragment, Using the Right Word, Comma (Appositive)**

A very popular desert in the Hispanic world flan a baked custard with caramel topping.

℮ **Capitalization, Comma (Other)**

Mexico is bordered by the pacific ocean and the gulf of california on the South and West and it is bordered by the gulf of mexico and the caribbean sea on the East.

℮ **Hyphen, Comma (Unnecessary), Adverb Form, Using the Right Word**

Venus appears extreme bright in the sky, because it's 20 mile thick cloud cover reflects three fourths of the light, that strikes it.

Corrected Sentences

℮ **Comma (Other), Numbers, Spelling, Colon, Hyphen, Article**

"Diamond Jim" Brady, ~~a~~ *an* American businessman, once ate the following for dinner*,* ~~6~~ *six* *:*

lobsters*,* ~~2~~ *two* ducks*,* ~~30~~ *thirty* oysters*,* a sirloin steak*,* ~~vegtables~~ *vegetables* ~~2~~ *two* quarts of orange juice*,* several

pastries*,* and a ~~2~~ *two-* pound box of candy.

℮ **Verb (Tense), Capitalization, Comma (Other), Using the Right Word**

Nellie Bly was a famous Investigative(*i*) Reporter(*r*) ~~whom~~ *who exposed* ~~exposes~~ american(*A*) slums*,*

sweatshops*,* jails*,* and insane asylums in the late 1800s.

℮ **Sentence Fragment, Using the Right Word, Comma (Appositive)**

A very popular ~~desert~~ *dessert* in the Hispanic world*,* flan*,* *is* a baked custard with caramel

topping.

℮ **Capitalization, Comma (Other)**

Mexico is bordered by the pacific(*P*) ocean(*O*) and the gulf(*G*) of california(*C*) on the South(*s*) and

West(*w*)*,* and it is bordered by the gulf(*G*) of mexico(*M*) and the caribbean(*C*) sea(*S*) on the East(*e*).

℮ **Hyphen, Comma (Unnecessary), Adverb Form, Using the Right Word**

Venus appears ~~extreme~~ *extremely* bright in the sky~~,~~ because ~~it's~~ *its* 20*-*mile*-*thick cloud cover

reflects three*-*fourths of the light~~,~~ that strikes it.

A Big Eater

Comma (Appositive), Comma Splice, Colon, Spelling, Comma (Other), Abbreviation, Capitalization, Sentence Fragment, Numbers, Verb (Tense), Using the Right Word, Plurals

1   "Diamond Jim" Brady a multimillionaire railroad tycoon was as well known

2   for his appetite as for his ability to make money, a typical breakfast for Jim might

3   include the following eggs steak, fried potatos, grits, bacon, muffins, pancakes and a

4   gallon of O.J. At dinner, which he often ate at rector's, an expensive N.Y.

5   restaurant. Diamond Jim might have three dozen oysters, two bowls of turtle soup

6   and 6 crabs for an appetizer. Space does not allow a listing of all he eats for

7   dinner. For desert he typicly ate a plateful of cakes and a 2-lb. box of candy.

8   Resterant owners called him one of the best 25 customers they ever had.

Sentence Combining

Combine the sentences that begin in lines 6 and 7 using a **coordinating conjunction**. (See page 734 in *Write Source* for an example and a list of coordinating conjunctions.) Write your combined sentence below.

_____

_____

_____

_____

Corrected Paragraph

◎ Comma (Appositive), Comma Splice, Colon, Spelling, Comma (Other), Abbreviation, Capitalization, Sentence Fragment, Numbers, Verb (Tense), Using the Right Word, Plurals

1   "Diamond Jim" Brady, a multimillionaire railroad tycoon, was as well known

2   for his appetite as for his ability to make money. A typical breakfast for Jim might

3   include the following: eggs, steak, fried *potatoes* potatos, grits, bacon, muffins, pancakes, and a

4   gallon of *orange juice.* O.J. At dinner, which he often ate at Rector's, an expensive *New York* N.Y.

5   restaurant, Diamond Jim might have three dozen oysters, two bowls of turtle soup,

6   and *six* 6 crabs for an appetizer. Space does not allow a listing of all he *ate* eats for

7   dinner. For *dessert* desert he *typically* typicly ate a plateful of cakes and a *two-pound* 2 lb. box of candy.

8   *Restaurant* Resterant owners called him one of the best 25 customers they ever had.

◎ **Sentence Combining**
Combine the sentences that begin in lines 6 and 7 using a **coordinating conjunction**. (See page 734 in *Write Source* for an example and a list of coordinating conjunctions.) Write your combined sentence below.

Space does not allow a listing of all he ate for dinner, but for dessert he typically

ate a plateful of cakes and a two-pound box of candy.

Set 27: Mixed Review

@ Subject-Verb Agreement, Apostrophe, Double Negative, Capitalization

I didnt never know that Jupiters mass are 2.5 times the combined mass of the rest of

the planets in the Solar System.

@ Abbreviation, Numbers, Capitalization, Verb (Tense), Comma (Appositive)

The first man in space yuri gagarin made a single orbit of the planet earth and

reaches an altitude of one hundred eighty-eighty mi.

@ Comma (Other), Numbers, Using the Right Word, Abbreviation

People think the amount of emigrants arriving in the U.S. is large today but between

1880 and 1920, 23,000,000 emigrants came into this country.

@ Using the Right Word, Subject-Verb Agreement, Pronoun-Antecedent Agreement,
Run-On Sentence

Gazelles are adopted to dry climates it needs no water since they get all the moisture

they need from solid food.

@ Run-on Sentence, Using the Right Word, Comma (Other), Numbers

Brown rats double there population every one hundred years humans on the other

hand now double there population every 47 years or less.

Corrected Sentences

@ **Subject-Verb Agreement, Apostrophe, Double Negative, Capitalization**

I didn̦t ~~never~~ know that Jupiter̦s mass ~~are~~ *is* 2.5 times the combined mass of the rest of the planets in the ₷olar ₷ystem.

@ **Abbreviation, Numbers, Capitalization, Verb (Tense), Comma (Appositive)**

The first man in space, ₙ ¥uri ₲agarin ₙ made a single orbit of the planet €arth and *reached* ~~reaches~~ an altitude of ~~one hundred eighty-eighty~~ *188* ~~mi.~~ *miles.*

@ **Comma (Other), Numbers, Using the Right Word, Abbreviation**

People think the *number* ~~amount~~ of *immigrants* ~~emigrants~~ arriving in the ~~U.S.~~ *United States* is large today ₙ but between 1880 and 1920, *23 million immigrants* ~~23,000,000 emigrants~~ came into this country.

@ **Using the Right Word, Subject-Verb Agreement, Pronoun-Antecedent Agreement, Run-On Sentence**

Gazelles are *adapted* ~~adopted~~ to dry climates ₍ *they need* ~~it needs~~ no water since they get all the moisture they need from solid food.

@ **Run-on Sentence, Using the Right Word, Comma (Other), Numbers**

Brown rats double *their* ~~there~~ population every ~~one hundred~~ *100* years ⊙ ℋumans ₙ on the other hand ₙ now double *their* ~~there~~ population every 47 years or less.

Passing the Eye Test on Ellis Island

1   Between 1880 and 1920, 23,000,000 emigrants came to the United States.

2   Between immigrants ellis island was known as "Heartbreak Island". Two doctors

3   from the United States health service examined the immigrants. The first looked

4   for physical and mental defects, the second looked for diseases espeshily for

5   simptoms of trachoma a contagious eye disease. Because trachoma was responsable

6   for more than half of the medical rejections. The second doctor was greatly feared.

7   As emigrants waited in a barnlike hall in lines seperated by iron gates, the eye

8   doctor would pull an eyelid up and peer at the underside for any sign of diseise.

9   Then the doctor would either wave the individual on. Or pull them aside for

10   farther testing.

Ⓔ **Sentence Combining**
Combine the sentences that begin in lines 7 and 8 using a **series of phrases**. (See page 610.2 in *Write Source* for an example.) Write your combined sentence below.

_____

_____

_____

_____

Corrected Paragraph

Spelling, Comma (Appositive), Capitalization, Using the Right Word, Sentence Fragment, Comma (Other), Numbers, Quotation Marks, Pronoun-Antecedent Agreement, Comma Splice

1 Between 1880 and 1920, ~~23,000,000 emigrants~~ *23 million immigrants* came to the United States.

2 ~~Between~~ *Among* immigrants, ~~e~~llis ~~i~~sland (*E*, *I*) was known as "Heartbreak Island"⌐ Two doctors

3 from the United States ~~h~~ealth ~~s~~ervice (*H*, *S*) examined the immigrants. The first looked

4 for physical and mental defects; the second looked for diseases, ~~espeshily~~ *especially* for

5 ~~simptoms~~ *symptoms* of trachoma, a contagious eye disease. Because trachoma was ~~responsable~~ *responsible*

6 for more than half of the medical rejections, ~~t~~*T*he second doctor was greatly feared.

7 As ~~emigrants~~ *immigrants* waited in a barnlike hall in lines ~~seperated~~ *separated* by iron gates, the eye

8 doctor would pull an eyelid up and peer at the underside for any sign of ~~diseise~~ *disease*.

9 Then the doctor would either wave the individual on ~~o~~*o*r pull ~~them~~ *him or her* aside for

10 ~~farther~~ *further* testing.

Sentence Combining

Combine the sentences that begin in lines 7 and 8 using a **series of phrases**. (See page 610.2 in *Write Source* for an example.) Write your combined sentence below.

As immigrants waited in a barnlike hall in lines separated by iron gates, the eye

doctor would pull an eyelid up, hold it up, then peer at the underside for any sign

of disease.

Set 28: Mixed Review

◉ Using the Right Word, Adjective Form, Spelling

Drinking ocean water may quickly make you feel badly because the additional salt throws off the delakit balance of salt and water in your body.

◉ Pronoun-Antecedent Agreement, Comma Splice, Plurals, Using the Right Word, Numbers, Subject-Verb Agreement

Mayflys live only 6 hours, it lies eggs that take 3 years to hatch.

◉ Article, Comma (Other), Subject-Verb Agreement, Spelling, Using the Right Word

A orchestra is typicly made up of string percussion woodwind and brass sections and are lead by a conductor.

◉ Sentence Fragment, Comma (Appositive), Subject-Verb Agreement, Capitalization

Piranha fish found in the waters of Eastern and Central South America swims and attacks. In schools of up to 1,000.

◉ Comma (Other), Using the Right Word, Comma (Nonrestrictive Phrase or Clause)

The town of Rugby North Dakota which lays about 45 miles from the Canadian border is the geographical center of North America.

Corrected Sentences

◉ **Using the Right Word, Adjective Form, Spelling**

Drinking ocean water ~~may~~ *can* quickly make you feel ~~badly~~ *bad* because the additional salt throws off the ~~delakit~~ *delicate* balance of salt and water in your body.

◉ **Pronoun-Antecedent Agreement, Comma Splice, Plurals, Using the Right Word, Numbers, Subject-Verb Agreement**

~~Mayflys~~ *Mayflies* live only ~~6~~ *six* hours, *yet they lay* ~~it lies~~ eggs that take ~~3~~ *three* years to hatch.

◉ **Article, Comma (Other), Subject-Verb Agreement, Spelling, Using the Right Word**

~~A~~ *An* orchestra is ~~typiely~~ *typically* made up of string, percussion, woodwind, and brass sections and ~~are~~ *is* ~~lead~~ *led* by a conductor.

◉ **Sentence Fragment, Comma (Appositive), Subject-Verb Agreement, Capitalization**

Piranha, fish found in the waters of *e*Eastern and *c*Central South America, ~~swims~~ *swim* and ~~attacks~~ *attack* ~~In~~ *in* schools of up to 1,000.

◉ **Comma (Other), Using the Right Word, Comma (Nonrestrictive Phrase or Clause)**

The town of Rugby, North Dakota, which ~~lays~~ *lies* about 45 miles from the Canadian border, is the geographical center of North America.

Don't Drink the (Ocean) Water

@ Quotation Marks, Punctuation (Title), Apostrophe, Nonstandard Language, Comma (Other),
Rambling Sentence, Plurals, Comma Splice, Indefinite Pronoun Reference, Capitalization

1   Water, water, everywhere, and not a drop to drink, says the poet in the

2 famous poem The Rime of the ancient Mariner but whats the big problem with

3 drinking ocean water anyways? The human body needs just the right concentration

4 of water and salt to be healthy and your kidnies keep water and salt in balance

5 and when you eat salted peanuts for example you need to drink more water so

6 you can flush on out the excess salt. Drinking salty ocean water may satisfy your

7 thirst for a moment. However, it will soon make you thirstier. Ocean water has so

8 much salt in it that the salt-to-water balance in your kidnies is quickly thrown off,

9 if you keep this up, you will soon be mad with unquenchable thirst.

@ Sentence Combining
Combine the sentence that begins in line 6 and the first sentence that begins in line 7
using an **introductory clause**. (See page 610.3 in *Write Source* for an example.) Write your
combined sentence below.

_____

_____

_____

_____

Corrected Paragraph

@ Quotation Marks, Punctuation (Title), Apostrophe, Nonstandard Language, Comma (Other),
Rambling Sentence, Plurals, Comma Splice, Indefinite Pronoun Reference, Capitalization

1   "Water, water, everywhere, and not a drop to drink," says the poet in the

2   famous poem "The Rime of the Ancient Mariner," but what's the big problem with

3   drinking ocean water ~~anyways~~ *anyway*? The human body needs just the right concentration

4   of water and salt to be healthy, and your ~~kidnies~~ *kidneys* keep water and salt in balance.

5   ~~and~~ *W*hen you eat salted peanuts, for example, you need to drink more water so

6   you can flush ~~on~~ out the excess salt. Drinking salty ocean water may satisfy your

7   thirst for a moment. However, it will soon make you thirstier. Ocean water has so

8   much salt in it that the salt-to-water balance in your ~~kidnies~~ *kidneys* is quickly thrown off.

9   *I*f you keep ~~this up~~ *drinking ocean water*, you will soon be mad with unquenchable thirst.

@ **Sentence Combining**
Combine the sentence that begins in line 6 and the first sentence that begins in line 7
using an **introductory clause**. (See page 610.3 in *Write Source* for an example.) Write your
combined sentence below.

Although drinking salty ocean water may satisfy your thirst for a moment, it will

soon make you thirstier.

Set 29: Mixed Review

@ **Apostrophe, Shift in Construction, Hyphen, Italics (Underlining), Capitalization, Commas**

Bonnies and Clydes last car was a tan colored 1934 V-8 deluxe that the manufacturer calls Desert Sand.

@ **Capitalization, Spelling, Article, Verb (Tense), Verb (Irregular)**

The north american indian langwages were unwrote until 1821, when a cherokee named sequoyah develops a 80-character alphabet for his native langwage.

@ **Sentence Fragment, Using the Right Word, Pronoun Usage**

While he was in prison. Malcolm X enlarged his vocabulary and learned hisself many things by copying the dictionary, page by page.

@ **Capitalization, Hyphen, Comma (Appositive)**

In 1875, captain Matthew Webb a 27 year old master of an english ship became the first person to swim the English channel.

@ **Run-On Sentence, Using the Right Word, Subject-Verb Agreement**

Spiders and ladybugs both eat other pesky bugs the former eats mosquitoes, while the later eats aphids.

Corrected Sentences

@ **Apostrophe, Shift in Construction, Hyphen, Italics (Underlining), Capitalization, Commas**

Bonnie
~~Bonnies~~ and Clyde's last car was a tan-colored, 1934 V-8 deluxe that the manufacturer

called
~~calls~~ <u>Desert Sand</u>.

@ **Capitalization, Spelling, Article, Verb (Tense), Verb (Irregular)**

N   *A*   *I*   *languages*   *unwritten*   *C*
The north american indian ~~langwages~~ were ~~unwrote~~ until 1821, when a cherokee

S   *developed an*   *language*
named sequoyah ~~develops a~~ 80-character alphabet for his native ~~langwage~~.

@ **Sentence Fragment, Using the Right Word, Pronoun Usage**

taught himself
While he was in prison, Malcolm X enlarged his vocabulary and ~~learned hisself~~ many

things by copying the dictionary, page by page.

@ **Capitalization, Hyphen, Comma (Appositive)**

C   *E*
In 1875, captain Matthew Webb, a 27-year-old master of an english ship, became the

C
first person to swim the English channel.

@ **Run-On Sentence, Using the Right Word, Subject-Verb Agreement**

eat
Spiders and ladybugs both eat other pesky bugs; the former ~~eats~~ mosquitoes, while the

latter eat
~~later eats~~ aphids.

The Dictionary and Malcolm X

Ⓔ Capitalization, Pronoun Usage, Using the Right Word, Comma (Other), Comma Splice, Spelling, Comma (Nonrestrictive Phrase or Clause), Quotation Marks, Sentence Fragment, Verb (Tense)

1   In prison, Malcolm X discovered the teachings of Elijah Muhammad and

2 joined the black muslims. He became increasingly frustrated by his lack of

3 education. His inability to express hisself good in words also frustrated him.

4 To learn himself Malcolm began copying the dictionary page by page, after copying

5 the first page which took him all day he discovers to his delight that he

6 remembered much of what he had copied. The dictionary is like a minature

7 encyclopedia wrote Malcolm in his autobiography. Eventually, he copied the entire

8 dictionary. And started on the road to reading and learning that made him an

9 eloquent speaker about the issues facing african americans.

Ⓔ **Sentence Combining**
Combine the sentences that begin in lines 2 and 3 using a **coordinating conjunction**. (See page 734 in *Write Source* for an example and a list of coordinating conjunctions.) Write your combined sentence below.

_____

_____

_____

_____

Corrected Paragraph

@ Capitalization, Pronoun Usage, Using the Right Word, Comma (Other), Comma Splice, Spelling,
Comma (Nonrestrictive Phrase or Clause), Quotation Marks, Sentence Fragment, Verb (Tense)

1   In prison, Malcolm X discovered the teachings of Elijah Muhammad and

                    B   *M*
2   joined the black muslims. He became increasingly frustrated by his lack of

                                       himself well
3   education. His inability to express ~~hisself good~~ in words also frustrated him.

       teach   *A*
4   To ~~learn~~ himself, Malcolm began copying the dictionary page by page, after copying
                      ,

                                           discovered
5   the first page, which took him all day, he ~~discovers~~ to his delight that he
              ,   ,

                                                              miniature
6   remembered much of what he had copied. "The dictionary is like a ~~minature~~

                    "
7   encyclopedia, wrote Malcolm in his autobiography. Eventually, he copied the entire
               ,

                a
8   dictionary. And started on the road to reading and learning that made him an

                                    A   *A*
9   eloquent speaker about the issues facing african americans.

@ **Sentence Combining**
Combine the sentences that begin in lines 2 and 3 using a **coordinating conjunction**. (See
page 734 in *Write Source* for an example and a list of coordinating conjunctions.) Write your
combined sentence below.

He became increasingly frustrated by his lack of education and his inability to

express himself well in words.

Set 30: Mixed Review

@ Comma (Other), Colon, Capitalization

The following nine Presidents never went to college Washington, Jackson, Van Buren, Taylor, Fillmore, Lincoln, Johnson (Andrew), Cleveland and Truman.

@ Comma Splice, Using the Right Word, Comma (Nonrestrictive Phrase or Clause), Plurals, Capitalization

Trees whose existence we often take for granted are disappearing from american citys, they're loss should not be tolerated by citizens who care about clean air.

@ Using the Right Word, Subject-Verb Agreement, Comma (Other)

Automobile drivers on highways and country roads kills more animals then hunters do but drivers use roads every day while hunters kill animals only during a designated time period.

@ Comma (Other), Italics (Underlining), Comma (Appositive)

In the moviemaking business two important people are the grip the person in charge of the props and the gaffer the chief electrician.

@ Subject-Verb Agreement, Comma Splice, Apostrophe

The rhinoceros and the yellow tickbird is a perfect example of symbiosis, the tickbird gets its meals (and does the rhino a favor) by picking out and eating nasty parasites from the rhinoceros skin.

Corrected Sentences

@ **Comma (Other), Colon, Capitalization**

The following nine ~~P~~*p*residents never went to college[:] Washington, Jackson, Van Buren, Taylor, Fillmore, Lincoln, Johnson (Andrew), Cleveland[,] and Truman.

@ **Comma Splice, Using the Right Word, Comma (Nonrestrictive Phrase or Clause), Plurals, Capitalization**

Trees[,] whose existence we often take for granted[,] are disappearing from ~~a~~*A*merican ~~citys~~*cities*[.] *Their* ~~they're~~ loss should not be tolerated by citizens who care about clean air.

@ **Using the Right Word, Subject-Verb Agreement, Comma (Other)**

Automobile drivers on highways and country roads ~~kills~~*kill* more animals ~~then~~*than* hunters do[,] but drivers use roads every day while hunters kill animals only during a designated time period.

@ **Comma (Other), Italics (Underlining), Comma (Appositive)**

In the moviemaking business[,] two important people are the <u>grip</u>[,] the person in charge of the props[,] and the <u>gaffer</u>[,] the chief electrician.

@ **Subject-Verb Agreement, Comma Splice, Apostrophe**

The rhinoceros and the yellow tickbird ~~is~~*are* a perfect example of symbiosis[;] the tickbird gets its meals (and does the rhino a favor) by picking out and eating nasty parasites from the rhinoceros['] *(or)* ['s] skin.

Trees, Please!

@ Numbers, Using the Right Word, Comma (Unnecessary), Capitalization, Sentence Fragment, Quotation Marks, Subject-Verb Agreement, Plurals, Hyphen, Spelling

1   Trees are 1 of those things who's existence we take for granted, but a recent

2   usda (united states department of agriculture) report says that trees play a big

3   role. In keeping people and the environment healthy. Says researcher, Gregory

4   McPherson, they [trees] filter small particles and absorbs harmful gaseous

5   pollutants such as ozone and sulfur dioxide out of the air." Unfortunately, one

6   study found that in American citys only 1 tree is planted for every 4 who die or

7   is cut down. Besides reducing pollution and providing cool shade, trees are

8   beautiful and calming reminders of nature, especially to stressed out city dwellers.

9   Go hug a tree today. Its probly good for your health and the tree's well-being.

@ Sentence Combining
Combine the sentences that begin in line 9 using **correlative conjunctions**. (See page 734.2 in *Write Source* for an example; also see page 734 for a list of correlative conjunctions.) Write your combined sentence below.

_____

_____

_____

_____

Corrected Paragraph

@ Numbers, Using the Right Word, Comma (Unnecessary), Capitalization, Sentence Fragment, Quotation Marks, Subject-Verb Agreement, Plurals, Hyphen, Spelling

                                 one   *whose*
1   Trees are ~~1~~ of those things ~~who's~~ existence we take for granted, but a recent

   USDA *U*   *S*   *D*   *A*
2   ~~usda~~ (united states department of agriculture) report says that trees play a big

           i   *"*
3   role in keeping people and the environment healthy. Says researcher Gregory

                   "T   *absorb*
4   McPherson, they [trees] filter small particles and ~~absorbs~~ harmful gaseous

5   pollutants such as ozone and sulfur dioxide out of the air." Unfortunately, one

                                cities   *one*   *four that*
6   study found that in American ~~citys~~ only ~~1~~ tree is planted for every ~~4~~ ~~who~~ die or

     are
7   ~~is~~ cut down. Besides reducing pollution and providing cool shade, trees are

8   beautiful and calming reminders of nature, especially to stressed-out city dwellers.

                            It's probably
9   Go hug a tree today. ~~Its~~ ~~probly~~ good for your health and the tree's well-being.

@ **Sentence Combining**
   Combine the sentences that begin in line 9 using **correlative conjunctions**. (See page
   734.2 in *Write Source* for an example; also see page 734 for a list of correlative conjunctions.)
   Write your combined sentence below.

   Go hug a tree today for both your health and the tree's well-being.

   _____

   _____

   _____

DAILY WRITING PRACTICE

Writing Prompts   129

Each reproducible page contains a quotation, a
photograph or graphic, and space for students to write.
We suggest that students write freely and rapidly in
response to each prompt, recording ideas as they come
to mind, one after another. Writers may then share their
writing. They may choose to shape it into a finished
narrative or essay.

Show-Me Sentences   141

The Show-Me Sentences are starting points for brief
paragraphs or essays that help students practice the
important skill of showing in writing.

Sentence Modeling and Expanding   144

The Sentence Modeling section contains helpful
guidelines and sample sentences for students to follow as
they work to improve their writing style by imitating the
techniques that authors use.

> "Give the world
> the best you have,
> and the best will
> come back to you."

"Everyone
makes mistakes.
It is what
you do afterward
that counts."

> "Only mediocre people
> are always
> at their best."

> "Everyone is
> an exception."

"Doing what you like
is freedom;
liking what you do
is happiness."

"The race is not always to the swift but to those who keep on running."

"No one can make you feel inferior without your consent."

Life's little storms . . .

....

....

....

....

....

....

....

....

....

....

....

....

....

....

....

....

....

....

....

....

....

Seeing things differently . . .

....

....

....

....

....

....

....

....

....

....

....

....

....

....

....

My mind went blank!

My Worst Fear

....

....

....

....

....

....

....

....

....

....

....

....

....

....

....

_____ **is like a spider's web.**

Show-Me Sentences

Teachers from time immemorial have said to their students, "Your essay lacks details and examples" or "This idea is too general" or "Show, don't tell." We've even heard of a teacher who had a special stamp made because he became so tired of writing "Give more examples" on student writing. So how should this problem be approached? It's obvious that simply telling students to add more details and examples is not enough.

Here's one method that has worked for many students and teachers: Have students develop basic sentences—sentences that *tell*—into brief paragraphs or essays that *show*.

MODEL OF SHOW-ME WRITING

It was a wild night.
(Show-Me sentence)

Winds raged, removing the last leaves from the trees. Branches squeaked, protesting the wind's wildness. I rose out of my chair by the fire, donned a heavy coat, pushed the door open, and went out. The clouds scudded across the moon, darkening the night before racing on. I turned left and pushed against the wind. At times I tilted my head into the collar of my coat. I noticed the wild cat huddled beneath Mr. Booth's rose bushes. A shutter banged on the house for sale. Parts of a newspaper were trapped in the Olson's picket fence. Next, I turned right. Main Street's lamps swayed. The sign on the diner swung back and forth, creaking, doing some kind of wild improvisational dance. The wind had the string of plastic triangles at the used car lot sticking straight out. Martha, who had worked the late shift at the diner ever since I came to this town, said, "Been expecting you. Lovely, wild night. Right?"

Recommendations

Before you ask students to work on their own, develop a Show-Me sentence as a class. Start by writing the model sentence on page 141 on the board. Then have students volunteer specific details that give this basic thought some life. List these ideas on the board. Next, construct a brief paragraph on the board or overhead using some of these details. (Make no mention of the original sentence in your paragraph.) Discuss the results. Make sure that your students see how specific details help create a visual image for the reader. Compare the model on page 141 with the paragraphs your students developed.

■ Students should now be prepared to develop sentences. Upon completion of their writing, have pairs of students share the results of their work. Then ask for volunteers to share their writing with the entire class. (You may want to make transparencies of the strongest paragraphs for class discussions.)

■ Students should develop Show-Me paragraphs once a week for at least a month. Discussing the results of their writing helps students make a personal connection to the writing process.

Note: Remember to write when your students write. Show them you are a writer, too.

Evaluation

Have students reserve a section in their notebooks for their writing or compile their work in a folder. Students should regularly receive some type of performance score for their efforts. At the end of the unit, have them select one or two of their best examples to revise and submit for a thorough evaluation.

Enrichment

In *Writers in Training,* Rebekah Caplan developed an extensive program to help students produce Show-Me writing. She made the following suggestions:

■ Have your students turn general statements like *It's a small world* or *Accidents will happen* into a Show-Me paragraph.

■ Have them develop sentences like *Cats make better pets than dogs* into comparison and contrast paragraphs.

■ In addition, have students convert loaded statements like *Physical education should not be mandatory* or *I don't need a haircut* into opinion pieces.

Note: These variations may become more and more challenging. Most student writers, for example, have more difficulty supporting an opinion than they have illustrating the basic ideas behind a cliche.

Show-Me Sentences

The test was a snap.

My job is not as easy as it looks.

Suddenly, everything was perfectly still.

He never seems able to settle down.

Our portable _____ is not very portable.

The _____ seemed to drag on forever.

Our enthusiasm was gone.

I've never known anyone so dynamic.

The dog looked like a stray.

We threw out half the things in our _____ .

The food was barely edible.

She/He is a very outgoing person.

It was a great party.

The place was shaking.

The skiing/skating/swimming was great.

The _____ floated overhead.

The weather was perfect.

I had a bad cold.

_____ is much more interesting than _____ .

No one expected it to happen, but it did.

His/Her locker was a mess.

I felt that it would all work out fine.

The news spread quickly.

I felt like a pioneer.

Our locker room _____ .

We rented a cottage near the beach.

I know how to _____ .

There have been times when I _____ .

The only thing you can count on in life is change.

The rain fell and fell.

There's this cozy little coffeehouse.

The umpire yelled, "Play ball!"

Looking out the window, I saw . . .

My mind spins trying to keep track of everything.

We had a skimpy meal.

We had a feast.

To this day I can't remember what all the fuss was about.

I like the attic.

I had never seen a night so peaceful and still.

We were lost, and we were scared.

I cleaned my room.

I fell and broke my arm.

Sentence Modeling and Expanding

Readers often marvel at how effectively professional authors can expand a basic idea with engaging details. Inexperienced writers often envy this ability not realizing that they can imitate these expanding techniques. One of the easiest ways for students to add detail is to use **cumulative sentences.** Composing cumulative sentences is a technique that can be easily learned, adding power and rhythm to writing. It is a professional technique that changes writing for the better almost at once.

A cumulative sentence "accumulates" (gathers) details as it rolls along. A basic idea gathers greater precision as modifying words, phrases, and clauses are added. Student writers can learn to compose cumulative sentences by modeling their sentences after those written by professionals. (Refer to "Modeling Sentences" on pages 96 and 560 and information on expanding sentences on pages 97 and 541–542 in *Write Source.* See page 98 in *Writers INC* for more information and examples.)

SAMPLE CUMULATIVE SENTENCES

He [a weasel] *was ten inches long,* thin as a curve, a muscled ribbon, brown as fruitwood, soft-furred, alert.
(The main clause is in italics.)

—*Teaching a Stone to Talk,* Joan Aiken

STUDENT MODEL

Their basketball center was six foot, seven inches tall, upright as a skyscraper, a known star, sculpted by exercising, fierce-eyed, ready.

Recommendations

Here's how many teachers help their students write cumulative sentences.

- Point out the basic working parts— both the main clause plus the additions. (Use the list of model sentences on pages 146–147.) Be careful not to make your discussion too technical. Remember that students don't necessarily have to identify and label phrases and clauses. By imitating a model, they achieve their goal.

- Model several cumulative sentences as a class. Do this work on the board or on an overhead.

Note: "Model" means the new sentences should be similar in structure to the original ones, not identical. The content should be different. Also use different words and ideas.

- Ask students to find examples of cumulative sentences to share with class members. (Authors and sources should be identified.) Tell them to look for sentences that read smoothly, clearly, and rhythmically.

- When students are ready to work on their own, give them one or two cumulative sentences. Use sentences from the list included in this booklet or sentences the students have collected. Give them the first part of the class period (5–10 minutes) to do their work. On alternate days, spend class time sharing their model sentences. Students may put their sentences on the board or a transparency.

- Help students experiment with each sentence. Write it several ways, to recombine parts, to abandon one idea and select another. It is in the trying, the experimenting, and the doing that much can be learned.

- Encourage students to submit new cumulative sentences they find in books or magazines for future modeling practice.

Note: Students may be asked (perhaps required on occasion) to use cumulative sentences in their writing.

Evaluation

Students should compile their work in a notebook or folder. They should receive some type of performance score for their efforts. Bonus points could be awarded for writing extra sentences, for finding additional models, or for including cumulative sentences in their writing.

Other Expanding Techniques

Have your students expand brief, general ideas using the five methods listed below. (See page 95 in *Writers INC.*) A list of basic sentences can be found on page 148. A basic thought like *The coyote howls* could be expanded in the following ways:

> The coyote howls **eerily.**
> (Add an individual word.)

> The coyote howls eerily
> **with his head thrown back.**
> (Add a prepositional phrase.)

> The coyote howls eerily, his head thrown back, **making my scalp tingle.**
> (Add a participial—either an *-ing* or *-ed*—phrase.)

> The coyote howls, **which makes my scalp tingle,** echo in the full-moon night.
> (Add a relative clause.)

> The coyote howls **until other coyotes across the canyon join in.**
> (Add a subordinate clause.)

Note: Have students think in terms of the 5 W's and H—who? what? where? when? why? and how?—when they try to expand these basic thoughts.

Enrichment

- You might also approach sentence expanding more systematically. For example, in an initial series of sentences, you might have students add one or two modifiers after the main clause. From there, you might have them place modifiers before the main clause. Later, they can experiment with splitting the main clause with modifiers.

- Or you might focus on the different types of modifiers used to expand basic ideas. (See "Using Phrases" on pages 742 and 744 and "Using Clauses" on page 744 in *Write Source.* See pages 552–553 in *Writers INC.*)

- Since some of the professional sentences included in our list use metaphors and similes, student writers can learn how to bring a basic idea to life using these techniques. (See page 601 and "Use Metaphors" on page 49. See examples of similes on pages 544 and 601 in *Write Source.* See pages 126 and 256 in *Writers INC* for examples of similes.)

Sentences for Modeling

Note: The main clause in each cumulative sentence below is in italics.

First there was the penicillum, a brush made of animal hair, a tool the Romans used to paint and to draw, an ancestor of our pencil.

It was the "cutting room," a room set up by Mother, a place where we could go to paste, cut, read, make scrapbooks, paint, write, and wonder.

Whenever Grandmother gave a dinner party, *she set the table the day before,* a masterpiece of sparkling glass and silver, white Irish linen, napkins large enough to use as scarves, and each guest's name on a thin glass placard standing in a tiny glass holder.

The men worked by the hour, the day, or until the hay was stacked, the fencing done, receiving their pay in cash.

Aromas we had known all our lives, aromas of lilacs and freshly mown grass and burning leaves, *vanished.*

She always wore a big coat with pockets bulging with crackers for the pigeons, bread for the geese, and peanut butter with banana sandwiches for herself.

There was no fire to be seen, only clouds of smoke and Mr. Prothero standing in the middle of them, waving his slipper as though he were conducting.
—*A Child's Christmas in Wales,* Dylan Thomas

The monster jigged and joggled, nodding its head, flopping all its prickles and plates.
—*The Moon's Revenge,* Joan Aiken

He was up the steps and in the small vestibule in no time, pressing the bell under the card that said "Mrs. Ulgine Barrows."
—"The Catbird Seat," James Thurber

We slid the boxcar door wide open at dawn to see a vast prairie, pale gold in the east, dark in the west.
—"On Running Away," John Keats

Sentences for Modeling

Note: The main clause in each cumulative sentence below is in italics.

The hotel lobby was a dark, derelict room, narrow as a corridor, and seemingly without air.

> —"Total Eclipse," Annie Dillard

An entire building had been constructed to quarantine them on their return, a species of hospital dormitory, gallery and laboratory for the moon rocks.

> —"The Psychology of Astronauts," Norman Mailer

My fingers a-tremble, *I complied,* smelling the fresh leather and finding an official-looking document inside.

> —*Invisible Man,* Ralph Ellison

Staring at the unblemished blue of the sky, listening to the children shout, "Rise, Sally rise, wipe your pretty eyes," *I turned that question over in my mind.*

> —*The Friends,* Rose Guy

I stand in the ghetto classroom—"the guest speaker"—attempting to lecture on the mystery of the sounds of our words to rows of diffident (hesitant) students.

> —"The Achievement of Desire," Richard Rodriguez

Soon the men began to gather, surveying their own children, speaking of planting and rain, tractors and taxes.

> —"The Lottery," Shirley Jackson

The candidate swings neatly to [the] left, hands raised, two forefingers of each hand making the victory salute.

> —"The Twenty-Ninth Republican Convention," Gore Vidal

A thrifty homemaker, wife, mother of three, *she also did all of her own cooking.*

> —"The Little Store," Eudora Welty

They'll honk nonstop for 10 minutes at a time, until the horns get tired and out of breath.

Basic Sentences to Expand

Note: Some of the following sentences already contain an adjective, an adverb, or a prepositional phrase. Students will be challenged to add specific details to these sentences. If they choose, students may change the pronouns and names.

The elevator door slid open.

The doctor came into the waiting room.

He forgot to water the plants.

We were afraid of the dark street.

The dog seemed huge (mean, scraggly, lovable, friendly).

The sky darkened.

The sky cleared.

We camped in the high country.

The fog made driving dangerous.

He liked his eggs over easy.

Some people are afraid of clowns.

She stooped to pick up the penny.

Turn the page.

My favorite apple is an Empire (Delicious, McIntosh, _____).

Read the poem.

My brother tried to bake a pie.

It started to snow.

I didn't want to ski.

We looked across the valley.

That kid is a bull rider.

The bull's name is Crooked Horn.

Jennison stood on the balcony.

The waves crashed against the seawall.

The black cat always sits in that window.

A piece of information can change your life.

She could feel her heart pounding.

The breeze from the Pacific rippled the curtains.

The classroom hummed with a Friday afternoon excitement.

She finds it funny.

The news makes me anxious.

His face reddened.

The cell phone rang.

A winter wind rattled the windows.

Her footsteps slowed.

Smithy biked 100 miles today.

The fingers of her right hand curled and uncurled.

Ms. Parso sped down the street.

Slow-moving traffic clogged the road.

JOURNALS AND LEARNING LOGS

Journals and Learning Logs   150

Whether students are writing in personal daily journals or processing their reading and classroom experiences in learning logs, they'll find helpful guidelines on the following pages.

Note: See pages 4, 5, 408–409, 419, 433, 445, and 455 in *Write Source* and pages 131–134 and 416–417 in *Writers INC.*

Writing Topics   154

A list of more than 100 high-interest writing topics provides students with ideas for exploratory freewriting. The topics are organized according to themes high school students find important.

Note: The writing guidelines and topics on the following pages can be reproduced for student use.

Guidelines for Keeping a Daily Journal

Your journal can be whatever you want it to be. Think of it as **a snapshot album**, and you are a roving photographer capturing life. Create portraits and landscapes. Or think of your journal as **a time capsule** in which you save important dates, events, and "keepsakes."

1. **Enjoy yourself . . .** Find a comfortable place to write and begin writing. Don't be afraid to experiment. Vary the type of writing you do—clustering, imaginary dialogues, lists, unsent letters, parodies, want ads, and so on. Find a new place to write if your writing starts to grow stale.

2. **Write whatever you like . . .** whatever is on your mind. This is your personal journal. (Use the list of writing ideas on page 584–585 of *Write Source* when you can't think of anything to write about.)

3. **Get into a writing routine and stick to it . . .** Write at least three or four times a week, ideally at the same time each day.

4. **Try writing nonstop . . .** This is how you get the most mileage out of your writing. Your goal should be to write for at least 10 minutes at a time. And try to write naturally and honestly, as if your writing were one-half of a conversation with a reader you know or one you invent.

5. **Keep it going . . .** If you draw a blank during a particular entry, write "I'm drawing a blank" until something comes to mind. The key to journal writing is to keep the ideas flowing.

6. **Discover . . .** The real satisfaction in keeping a journal is making new discoveries. Make that your goal. Don't be overly concerned about the appearance of your writing. It obviously should be legible, but it doesn't have to be (and shouldn't be) a tidy, error-free essay.

7. **Underline ideas . . .** in your journal that you like. Maybe a particular idea helped clarify your thinking on a certain issue or brought a whole new way of thinking to mind. Continue exploring interesting ideas in future entries or in your assigned writing.

8. **Push an idea as far as you can . . .** But, if an unrelated idea bumps into your writing, go with it. It might lead to a more exciting line of thinking.

9. **Experiment in your writing . . .** Write like your favorite author or like your best friend. Write in a foreign language. Follow your senses and write what you hear, see, smell, feel, or taste.

10. **Develop ideas you really like into more polished pieces . . .** personal narratives, poems, plays, letters, dialogues, and so on. (Share them with your friends.)

Journal Writing Ideas

Writing is like other forms of exercise. It is sometimes hard to get up the energy to begin, but once you do, you feel much better for it. Your own experiences will trigger a number of potential writing ideas. If, however, nothing personal moves you to write, try picking up on the experiences of a friend, classmate, or family member; on something you have read in the newspaper; or, perhaps, on something that catches your eye as you sit with pen in hand. On those occasions when you still draw a blank, consider using the basics-of-life list and the open-ended sentences that follow for possible starting points for your writing.

Basics-of-Life List

This list identifies the major categories into which those things humans need to live a full life are divided; it also provides an endless variety of journal writing possibilities. Consider the first category, clothing. It could lead to a journal entry about

the clothes you are wearing or the clothes you wish you were wearing.

the wardrobe of a friend, classmate, or family member.

your all-time favorite piece of clothing or something you always hated to wear.

past, present, and future fashion trends.

clothing as a statement (the "we are what we wear" idea).

the clothes you were wearing when . . .

clothing and peer pressure.

blue jeans or blue suits: What will you be wearing in 10 years?

school dress codes and on and on and on.

- clothing
- housing
- food
- communication
- exercise
- education
- family
- friends
- purpose/goals
- love
- measurements
- senses

- machines
- intelligence
- history/records
- agriculture
- environment
- land/property
- work/occupation
- community
- science
- plants/vegetation
- freedom/rights
- energy

- rules/laws
- tools/utensils
- heat/fuel
- natural resources
- personality/identity
- recreation/hobby
- trade/money
- literature/books
- entertainment
- health/medicine
- art/music
- faith/religion

Open Ends

The following list of open-ended sentences provides a number of writing possibilities. The most obvious way to use this list is to complete one of the open-ended sentences and then write about it to see what you can discover. Write as freely and spontaneously as you can and push yourself to explore this statement from a number of different angles.

You might also focus on one particular open-ended sentence and complete it in as many ways as you can in rapid-fire fashion. A variation of this type of writing would be to alternate responses with a friend or classmate and work from each other's ideas. You might also consider completing one of these sentences from another point of view. Write from the perspective of a senior citizen, a teacher, a doctor, a person from the past, an object, or a color and see what develops.

Note: The last three ideas in the following list will lead to comparison writing: comparing different periods in your life, different points of view, different courses of action.

> *I wonder . . .*
>
> *I hope . . .*
>
> *I wish . . .*
>
> *I was afraid when . . .*
>
> *If only . . .*
>
> *I would like to suggest . . .*
>
> *I have learned that . . .*
>
> *I want to ask . . .*
>
> *I'm beginning to wonder . . .*
>
> *I was surprised to find that . . .*
>
> *Now that I think of it, I . . .*
>
> *I want to make a contract with myself to . . .*
>
> *I need help with . . .*
>
> *I never thought I would see the day when . . .*
>
> *I was once _____ , but now I am _____ .*
>
> *They say _____ , but my experience tells me _____ .*
>
> *I decided to _____ instead of _____ , and it changed everything.*

Special Note: Consider reserving one-half of your journal for your personal writing, the other half for your learning log. Or, better yet, use your daily journal for your personal writing and another notebook for your learning log.

Guidelines for Keeping a Learning Log

A learning log is a notebook where you can "dig deeper" into what you are learning. Use the following suggestions to become more involved in your class discussions, group projects, experiments, and reading assignments. Also see pages 408–409, 419, 433, 445, and 455 in *Write Source* and pages 416–419 in *Writers INC*.

1. **Write about class activities . . .** anything from a class discussion to an important exam. Consider what was valuable, confusing, interesting, humorous, and so on.

2. **Explain new ideas and concepts . . .** Consider how this new information relates to what you already know.

3. **Evaluate your course work in a particular class . . .** Consider your strengths, your weaknesses, your relationship with members of the class.

4. **Discuss your course work with a particular audience . . .** a young child, a foreign exchange student, an object, a classmate, an alien from another planet, a mentor, a pet, someone or something of your choice.

5. **Question what you are learning . . .** Dig deeply into the importance of the concepts presented. Consider writing this in the form of a dialogue.

6. **Confront concepts that confuse you . . .** Back them into a corner until you better understand the problem. (Consider giving a copy of your thoughts to your teacher so that he or she has a better idea of how you and the class are doing.)

7. **Describe . . .** your assignments in your own words.

8. **Plan the activities for the next day's class . . .** Or develop a mock essay test. Make sure to answer one or more of the questions. (This is a very effective study method.)

9. **Keep a record of your thoughts . . .** and feelings during an extended lab or research assignment. This will help you evaluate your progress. And the ideas that develop in your log entries will often add new meaning to your work.

10. **Set aside a section in your log . . .** for a glossary of important and interesting vocabulary words. Use these words in your log entries.

Active Note Taking

An effective variation of the basic learning log is to record your thoughts and feelings alongside your course notes. Divide each page in your notebook in half. Use one side for traditional notes from lectures, discussions, and reading. Use the other side to react to these notes. This makes note taking an active, stimulating activity. Your responses could include the following:

- a reaction to a particular point you strongly agree or disagree with
- a question about a concept that confuses you
- a paraphrase (summary in your own words) of a difficult or complex idea
- a comment on what memory or feeling an idea brings to mind
- a discussion of the importance or significance of the material
- a reaction to an idea that confirms or questions a particular belief

Writing Topics

No other activity gets students into writing more effectively than personal journal writing. And no other writing activity is so easy to implement. Ask any teacher who has his or her students write in journals. All students need are journals and pens, time to write (at least 10 minutes every day), and encouragement to explore their minds. That's all it takes.

Recommendations

The lists of high-interest writing topics that follow provide your students with more than 100 starting points for their personal or journal writing. The topics are organized according to type and theme to make them easier to find and use.

Describe . . .

- a scorching-hot day
- a storm at sea
- an ant carrying a big crumb
- a deer sensing a hunter
- a homeless shelter
- the mall on a Saturday afternoon
- an obvious tourist
- children on a beach
- someone throwing a tantrum
- someplace you've never wanted to go
- feeling free

Describe someone . . .

- who always overreacts
- who follows the crowd
- who always knows the right thing to say
- who is a wallflower
- who intrudes on other people's lives
- who has noble qualities
- who is an e-friend you've never met
- who is moody
- who is egotistical
- who is brave
- who is unselfish
- who has overcome adversity
- who has learned a hard lesson

Remember . . .

- an action you've later regretted
- a fight you had with a friend
- a conversation in the lunchroom
- feeling trapped
- a practical joke someone played on you
- the funniest thing . . .
- a time a stranger helped you out
- getting away with something
- a childhood dream
- stealing bases in baseball

Imagine . . .

- life without computers
- being a teenager in your grandparents' time
- winning $5,000
- being able to make yourself invisible

My mind wonders . . .

- what it's like to be blind
- what it's like to be old
- what it's like to be homeless
- what it's like to be a teacher
- what it's like to live in a big city/the country
- what it would be like to be my pet

What do you think?
(Agree/Disagree)

- Silence is golden.
- Everyone should recycle.
- Bread is the most useful food.
- All Americans are free.
- Everyone should be allowed into college.
- All students should have art and music classes.
- Government employees should pay into the Social Security system.

Define . . .

- an ethical person
- the earliest Americans
- a modern-day Don Quixote
- peace
- friendship
- wealth
- efficiency
- a patriot
- a hero
- security

Discuss . . .

- the role of the elderly in our society
- what the American dream is today
- the U.S. president as a role model
- the role of sports in schools
- the role of childhood in our society
- the importance of good nutrition

Compare . . .

- a naive person/an uneducated person
- a book lover/a bookworm
- a morning person/a night person
- students of 1905/students of 2005
- an ideal American/a real American
- two people who are very alike
- an optimist/a pessimist
- silent sport/"noisy" sport
- public school/homeschooling

Can you tell me . . .

- the difference between frogs and toads?
- how national polls are taken?
- how to construct a ship in a bottle?
- why people imitate each other?
- the causes and effects of anger?
- why daydreaming makes some people happy?
- what motivates people to be courageous?
- how to avoid boredom?
- how to make schools safe?

A matter of debate . . .

- What are citizens' "rights" to privacy?
- What direction should be taken to develop future energy sources?
- How should the world's oceans be controlled?
- What impact will China and Asia have on U.S. job markets?

Edible Quotables (Food for Thought)

"Cautious, careful people always casting about to preserve their reputation or social standards never can bring about reform."
—Susan B. Anthony

"A clear conscience is often the sign of a bad memory."
—Steven Wright

"Being powerful is like being a lady. If you have to tell someone you are—you aren't."
—Margaret Thatcher

"I'm not confused; I'm just well mixed."
—Robert Frost

"Some people believe that holding on and hanging in there are signs of great strength. However, there are times when it takes much more strength to know when to let go—and then do it."
—Ann Landers

"You don't stop laughing because you grow old; you grow old because you stop laughing."
—Michael Pritchard

"The bitterest tears shed over graves are for words left unsaid and deeds left undone."
—Harriet Beecher Stowe

"When a thing is funny, search it carefully for a hidden truth."
—George Bernard Shaw

"You gain strength, courage, and confidence by every experience in which you really stop to look fear in the face."
—Eleanor Roosevelt

"There is nothing so fatal to character as half-finished tasks."
—David Lloyd George

"If you don't like something, change it. If you can't change it, change your attitude. Don't complain."
—Maya Angelou

"To know is nothing at all; to imagine is everything."
—Anatole France

"He who angers you conquers you."
—Elizabeth Kenny

"How much time we spend learning how to make a living, and how little time learning how to live."
—William James

"We cannot all do great things, but we can all do small things with great love."
—Mother Teresa

Proverbs

"Care, and not fine stables, makes a good horse."
—Danish proverb

"He who is outside his door has the hardest part of his journey behind him."
—Flemish proverb

"The best armor is to keep out of range."
—Italian proverb

"Turn your face to the sun and the shadows fall behind you."
—Maori proverb

"Whoever gossips to you will gossip about you."
—Spanish proverb

"When two elephants fight it is the grass that suffers."
—African proverb